AMARO

AMARO

THE SPIRITED WORLD OF
BITTERSWEET, HERBAL LIQUEURS

BRAD THOMAS PARSONS

WITH COCKTAILS, RECIPES,
AND FORMULAS

PHOTOGRAPHS BY ED ANDERSON

TEN SPEED PRESS
Berkeley

ZISSOU:
Hey, intern. Get me a Campari, will you?

INTERN:
On the rocks?

*Zissou snaps his fingers and gives
a "finger gun" salute.*

—WES ANDERSON AND NOAH BAUMBACH
The Life Aquatic with Steve Zissou

CONTENTS

INTRODUCTION

Sometimes when you walk into a bar for the very first time you immediately know that it's going to be one of your favorites. This was the case in Seattle when, in 2012, I stepped inside Barnacle, a narrow annex that you might mistake for the coat check next door to Renee Erickson's always-jammed Ballard restaurant, the Walrus and the Carpenter. This was my first visit to Barnacle, and I was there because of a two-hour wait (and the hostess stressed, a *true* two-hour wait) for a solo spot at the oyster bar next door. I settled into one of the fourteen stools lining the copper bar, and when they called my name two hours later I didn't want to leave.

Barnacle stocks more than forty different bottles of Italian amaro and thirty bottles of vermouth along with grappa and assorted herbal liqueurs. The beautiful wall of bottles dominates the entire back wall of the bar and, in true aperitivo style, customers are welcomed with a complimentary plate of Lay's potato chips.

I ordered one of my favorite cocktails, a Boulevardier (a kissing cousin to the gin-based Negroni but made with bourbon) from Barnacle co-owner David Little. He reached for the bottle of Bulleit rye (the one bottle of whiskey he keeps on hand for old-fashioneds), but swapped in the ruby-red, wine-based Cappelletti (which I had never tried) for the Campari and Punt e Mes for the traditional sweet vermouth. While I was in my own bitter reverie, sipping my Boulevardier, picking at my potato chips, and discussing the finer points of amaro with Little, the couple next to me wasn't in as good spirits. They weren't going to pass their two-hour wait without complaining about it, and pushing aside the perfectly curated cocktail menu, they methodically ordered a round of vodka tonics. I'm all for the customer being able to drink what they want, but I also believe in respecting (or at least acknowledging) the environment you're in when ordering (I'm not going to order a Boulevardier at a bowling alley). A world of possible aperitifs was at their disposal but there was no sense of adventure. Little made them their vodka tonics without judgment—using vodka from nearby Sound Spirits Distillery and a single-serve bottle of Fever-Tree tonic—but I couldn't help but stew over their lack of adventure. The man took a sip of his vodka tonic, finally looked over the room, then said to his date, "Look at all of these bottles of booze. I could not even begin to tell you what the fuck any of these are." They quickly finished their drinks and threw in the towel, moving on to another nearby restaurant where they wouldn't have such a long wait.

Amaro appreciation wasn't yet on this guy's radar, and it may never be. And truly, I'm sympathetic to his plight. Amaro is a category without many clearly defined boundaries, with a rich history that dates back over two hundred years. But within the last few years, amaro has transformed from stand-alone aperitif or end-of-meal digestif to being drafted into service by American bartenders as a key ingredient in inventive cocktails. Classic Italian amari like Meletti, Lucano, and Averna are shaking off the dust of the backbar to make their way center stage in high-profile bars and restaurants across the country, from Osteria Mozza in Los Angeles to Maialino in New York. And specialized bars devoted to amari are thriving—from Amor y Amargo in New York to Billy Sunday in Chicago to Barnacle in Seattle. The amaro shelf at many liquor stores is starting to grow in selection as the rise in amaro appreciation has encouraged importers and distributors to bring more international brands into the United States.

But this truly has been a recent phenomenon. In 2009, a mere three years before my visit to Barnacle, I was talking with bartender David Nelson about how he made rhubarb bitters using a sous vide method to speed up the infusion process when he reached behind the bar for a tall red-capped bottle of Zucca. "Check this out," he said, pouring out a taste of the burnt caramel–colored liqueur. Made in Milan since the 1860s, it's created from a proprietary blend of rhubarb, cardamom, bitter orange, and curative herbs based on principles of Chinese medicine. Smooth and woodsy with a hint of smoke, it was like nothing I had tried before. "Needless to say, we don't get many calls for it, but it's one of my favorites."

As cocktail trends go, what is first embraced by the brotherhood and sisterhood of bartenders will soon find its way across the bar to cocktail geeks before lighting up the radar of the general public. Today, Americans are learning to appreciate the taste of bitter in food and drinks—from bitter greens to chocolates to, yes, cocktails—which is why the diverse world of herbal, bittersweet liqueurs that fall under the umbrella of amaro is about to set off a loud, collective ping on drinkers' radars.

My passion for bitters serves as a natural through-line to exploring the world of amaro. When I was writing *Bitters*, the bracingly bitter Italian elixir Fernet-Branca was already an industry darling as the preferred shift drink among bartenders, but like many people, my first experience with amaro was the herbal German digestif Jägermeister. This college-bar staple, adorned with a noble stag on the cryptic label, is still typically served as an ice-cold shot and immediately hits you with a bitter buzz. Fittingly, Jägermeister is currently being revisited among select bartenders as something more than a vehicle to public drunkenness and more refined Jägermeister cocktails are popping up on menus.

Admittedly, I travel in the bitters-loving world of bartenders and cocktail aficionados, who are thrilled to obsess over matters such as pre-Prohibition-era aromatic bitters and nineteenth-century Italian liqueurs. Yet I hope *Amaro* can serve as a resource for any flustered lady or fellow who is intimidated by the bizarre bottles of booze on display behind the bar, just as it will be for the seasoned bartender or cocktail geek. With bartenders now getting calls for brands they weren't even carrying a few years ago, there is plenty of room for further education on the subject and, more important, demystification. Another key part of the culture of amaro is the notion of hospitality—the way it can symbolize the transition from workday into evening and serve as a soul-warming digestif. When I first moved to Brooklyn, my first dinner in the neighborhood after unpacking was at Frankies 457 in Carroll Gardens. After finishing a plate of cavatelli with spicy sausage, the bartender recommended their wine-stewed prunes with mascarpone for dessert. The simple dish delivered as promised, and so did the gratis glass of Averna he slid across the bar with a "welcome to the neighborhood" nod.

You may have to pour yourself your own glass of Averna, but consider this my "welcome to the book" nod. I remain so very grateful for all the readers and bartenders and industry professionals who embraced *Bitters*, and I hope you'll take this out for a bittersweet spin. Seeing *Bitters* travel around the country and spotted behind bars in Paris, Berlin, Tokyo, London, and beyond means, well, the world, to me. I can only hope that *Amaro* will be as well traveled among readers.

Stay bitter!

CHAPTER I

DEMYSTIFYING

AMARO

UNDERSTANDING AMARO

There's so much weight, history, and complexity packed into the word *amaro*. One thing that people can agree on is that *amaro* (plural: *amari*) is Italian for "bitter," but when it comes to the production, appreciation, and consumption of amaro, we're guided more by tradition than strict categorization and classification. Generally speaking, amaro refers to the collective class of Italian-made aromatic, herbal, bittersweet liqueurs traditionally served as a digestif after a meal. Amari are created by macerating and/or distilling bitter barks, herbs, seeds, spices, citrus peels, flowers, and other botanicals in a neutral spirit or wine that is then sweetened with a sugar syrup. Most amari are then rested for a period of time to help further balance the blend and some also undergo months or up to a year of additional aging in barrels for extra complexity. Common bittering agents used to make amaro include cinchona bark, gentian root, wormwood, and angelica root, along with additional ingredients ranging in number from a dozen to more than forty that can include herbs and spices like cardamom, chamomile, rhubarb, mint, orange peel, fennel, artichoke, licorice, eucalyptus, juniper, ginger, cardoon, clove, anise, saffron, and sage. Typically lower proof, between 16 and 40 percent alcohol, the bitterness scale can run from syrupy sweet to bone dry with a range of flavors from bright citrus to floral to vegetal to woodsy to mentholated to bracingly medicinal. While there are similarities to the ingredients used, the primary difference between amaro and cocktail bitters like Angostura and Peychaud's is that amaro is potable, meant to be consumed directly, while bitters are higher-proof and nonpotable and intended to be used as a flavoring agent applied in drops and dashes and not consumed directly on their own.

While Italy is the birthplace of amaro and home to the biggest selection of what's commercially available, the practice of serving a spirituous closer to the end of a rich meal isn't strictly an Italian affair. Technically, a digestif could be a glass of brandy, port, eau-de-vie, schnapps, or even scotch, but bitter and bittersweet herbal liqueurs purporting to aid digestion and well-being have been produced across western and central Europe for centuries: there's Underberg and Jägermeister in Germany; Gammel Dansk in Denmark; Unicum in Hungary; Becherovka in the Czech Republic; and aromatized and fortified aperitif wines such as Suze, Salers, and Avèze in France. And that's just to name a few of the many global brands available.

Millennia ago, ancient Greeks and Romans turned to blends of aromatic roots and botanicals for medicinal purposes, but the origins of amaro as we know it today can be traced back to medieval friars and monks in abbeys and monasteries across Italy, whose interest in alchemy and the unique restorative properties of herbs and botanicals led them to create bitter tonics. These secret formulas were preserved in a wine or alcohol base and used as an elixir to both stimulate the appetite and aid digestion. Many of these regional blends highlighted local ingredients, such as bitter oranges in Sicily and southern Italy and Alpine herbs and flowers in northern Italy, but the spice trade and Venice's key role in it opened the door to new, exotic herbs and spices to experiment with. Sugar was still an expensive ingredient, primarily due to the labor involved in producing it, so many examples of old-world amaro were more bitter than sweet, especially compared with many of today's current brands. John Troia, cofounder of Tempus Fugit Spirits, says, "Historic spirits are punctuated by big, bold, in-your-face flavors. There wasn't a lot of subtlety."

The beginning of the anticlericism movement in Italy forced many monasteries to cease production, and by the early nineteenth century, amaro's association with monasteries evolved into commercial production. After World War II, amaro had transitioned from a prescriptive aid sold by pharmacists or localized homemade versions to a commercial product purchased and consumed for pleasure.

YOU BITTER? YOU BET

Humans are born with a genetic predisposition to avoid bitter. Years of evolution have us hardwired to treat anything bitter as a potential toxin—so when your brain senses bitterness, it kick-starts the digestive system, activating the opening acts of saliva and gastric juices in an attempt to expel what you've just ingested. But this cycle also plays a role in why you have a sense of relief when you've had an amaro after a heavy meal. While your doctor won't likely endorse the prescriptive merits of a glass of Fernet-Branca to help you feel less bloated and distressed after a gut-busting meal, it's hard to deny the restorative effect of bittering agents and herbs as they course through your body. One of my favorite, and apt, descriptions of the impact a glass of amaro can have comes from *The Modern Gentleman* author Jason Tesauro, who summed it up like this in the *New York Times*: "After a decadent meal, amaro is like Harvey Keitel in *Pulp Fiction*. It's the cleaner that wipes away any evidence that you overdid it." Jennifer McLagan's award-winning book *Bitter: A Taste of the World's Most Dangerous Flavor, with Recipes* seems like a title Keitel's Winston "the Wolf" Wolfe might want to add to his home library. Discussing our built-in bitters early-warning system acquired at birth, McLagan writes, "It's a protective mechanism, as many bitter-tasting foods and liquids can be toxic, and even small doses are dangerous . . . As we age, we learn that not all bitter things are poisonous, and we come to appreciate a glass of beer, a gin and tonic, and coffee and tea." In the taste sensation lineup, bitter is the bad boy who gets asked to stay after class while sweet, sour, salty, and their friend umami get a pass. Bitter can save our lives, but once you've grown accustomed to it, it can be an acquired taste whose enjoyment can enhance your life tenfold. Italy is a country that traditionally embraces bitter food and drink, like bitter greens, anise-flavored sweets, and espresso, and children in Italy learn to like bitter as a flavor much younger compared with those in America, where a sweeter profile is more common.

THE TRICKY TAXONOMY OF AMARO

As Americans are learning to love their kale salad and other big, bold bitter flavors, the knee-jerk defensive mechanism toward bitter drinks is gradually being replaced with a new curiosity that can ultimately lead to the discovery of so many amari to try. But when one gets ready to jump down the bittersweet rabbit hole and explore the world of amaro, the first thing you realize is that, unlike whiskey, rum, wine, beer, and other spirits, there isn't a rule book when it comes to amaro production, classification, regulation, and even appreciation. The primary issue is the secrecy around the recipes. Many amaro producers are still family affairs, with the fourth, fifth, and sixth generations guarding their proprietary recipes with a level of secrecy reserved for Colonel Sanders's secret herbs and spices or the formula for Coca-Cola. Some of the younger-generation amaro makers are helping bring their business into the modern age through social media outreach and some transparency into the ingredients used to make their signature amaro. When I met with brothers Leonardo and Francesco Vena, representing the fourth generation of Amaro Lucano, which has been produced in Basilicata, Italy, since 1894, over drinks at the Milan bar Rita, they were adamant that a bittersweet liqueur can only be a true amaro if it's produced in Italy. Italy is the country that put amaro on the map, and other producers I met with, like Matteo Meletti, whose surname graces the bottle of his family's amaro, which has been made in Ascoli Piceno since 1870, feel just as strongly on the subject. He, along with other Italian amaro makers I spoke with, desires that a DOC (*Denominazione di Origine Controllata*) protection, the regulations employed by the Italian government to protect the historical origin and integrity of their country's culinary treasures like wine, cheese, and even Neopolitan pizza, be applied to amaro.

While I can appreciate that sentiment and the inherent sense of pride regarding amaro's proper birthplace, I feel that the bittersweet genie is already out of the bottle—and given amaro's increasing popularity with bartenders and cocktail afficiandos, there's no going back. I respect the traditions and customs of Italian-made amari, but just as my local Brooklyn pizzeria Lucali makes a beautiful Neopolitan-style pizza, there are quality producers of bittersweet liqueurs beyond Italy that maintain the standards set by Italian producers and should be able to call their product *amaro* without reservation.

But apart from region of origin, amaro as a category is still famously hard to define. Alex Bachman, a partner at Chicago's amaro-centric bar Billy Sunday, calls amaro a "broad and loosely defined category," and Avery Glasser of Bittermens once told me, "It's all a mess. The way I usually put it, under liqueurs you've got fruit, herbal, and bitter, with the difference between herbal and bitter being more about self-definition. But only France and Italy tend to define things as bitter liqueurs." Even more exasperating is that while *amaro* means "bitter," Italians call Campari and other aperitivo-style liqueurs that are meant to be enjoyed at the beginning of a meal a "bitter" (using the English word), which every Italian I've met insists is not the same as amaro (even though in America, Campari is shelved next to other amaro and considered an amaro by most bartenders). Red "aperitivo bitters" like Campari aren't the only source of confusion: Fernet-Branca is marketed as both an aperitif and a digestif, and lighter, gateway amari like Amaro Nonino Quintessentia, with its strong bitter orange and burnt caramel notes, are perfectly at home at the start or finish of a meal. Taylor Parsons, the beverage director at Los Angeles restaurant République, admits, "You can go kind of crazy with all of this, especially with Italians and their obsession with authenticity. You've got bitter things that work before a meal and bitter things that work after a meal." For Matteo Meletti, the key defining factor in what he considers amaro is timing: "It is all about the act of when you drink it—at the end of the meal. The ritual of it all is important."

Most would agree that fernet (which includes but is not limited to Fernet-Branca) is a subcategory or class of amaro, typically defined by common ingredients like aloe ferox, myrrh, and chamomile, but some say no, amaro is amaro, fernet is fernet. (For more on the origins and etymology of fernet, see page 51.) Even those common ingredients that loosely define what makes a fernet aren't strictly adhered to or regulated. That every bottle of amaro is a singular experience makes the category invigorating and open to exploration . . . but it's also challenging. Without strict classification, we're left with known styles of amaro, such as light (citrus-forward, lighter in color), medium (darker color, moderate alcohol, balanced bittersweet herb and citrus), Alpine (made with mountain herbs and flowers), fernet (very bitter, higher alcohol), carciofo (made with artichoke), rabarbaro (made with rhubarb), and tartufo (made with black truffles). While not strictly amari, the wine-based categories of vermouth and aromatized and fortified wines like quinquina are related to amaro and have more European Union regulations in place, but to cover that would require another book. Jackson Cannon, owner of Boston's the Hawthorne, says, "The traditions of vermouth run deeper. We don't get modern vermouth until the birth of amaro, but vermouth has a much longer history."

In an article on *Eater*, Alex Bachman expounds on the challenges and pleasures wrapped around the world of amaro when one takes a deeper dive into it: "In many ways the lack of structure can be the most frustrating facet with regard to studying amari, but likewise the most enticing. Think about it. Alcohol production for which a producer can literally use anything, from anywhere, to create the product they desire. It's one of the only platforms in which passionate craftsmen can express themselves in any way they want, unencumbered by government oversight. Amaro is a spirit that not only encourages but requires customers to become intimately familiar with each brand's methods and history."

I struggled wrapping my head around the best way to approach this. While it would be helpful to have distinctive classifications to help with the education and appreciation of amaro, the fact that the contents of every bottle is a whole world unto itself presents a pioneering, Wild West spirit that infuses my belief that, for the purpose of this book, I'm using the word *amaro* as a big bitter umbrella to cover the category of bittersweet, herbal liqueurs—whether their provenance is Italy, Germany, France, Chicago, or Charleston—filtered through my own American point of view. I was talking with my favorite outlaw barman in Brooklyn, Damon Boelte, on the topic and, in his own special way, he broke it down for me like this: "When you get down to the actual science of what it does, it's all the same. But in America we don't leave shit alone. We hit the gas pedal. We're not just taking a ride; we want to drive faster. You've got to pick and choose your battles, man. The lines are blurred on what you can or cannot do, but look at it this way, if a producer went out of their way to make it bitter, it's fair game."

APPRECIATING AMARO

In Italy, you may be offered dozens of different amari to choose from after a meal, including bottles from commercial producers as well as smaller, regional finds, and even signature blends made at the restaurant. In America, the art of the after-dinner drink is often reserved for a special occasion rather than something built into the ritual of the meal itself. The restaurant group run by Joe Bastianich, his mother Lidia Bastianich, and Mario Batali has been featuring a selection of amaro on their menu since 1999 at Lupa and continues the tradition at Babbo and Del Posto. This was before the selection of amaro available in the United States began to grow, as it has over the past few years. Many of those bottles were brought back directly from Italy and put on display behind the bar for show only, save for the occasional gratis pour to a VIP, regular, or industry friend.

Early American amaro enthusiasts include importer Eric Seed, called the "Indiana Jones of spirits," whose company Haus Alpenz has helped usher in aperitif wines like Bonal, Byrrh, and Cocchi Americano in the United States as well as amari like Cappelletti, Cardamaro, Elisir Novasalus, and Zucca Rabarbaro. And San Francisco bar owner and self-described "amaro hunter" Greg Lindgren was an early pioneer on the amaro trail through his travels in Italy with his wife Shelley Lindgren, the co-owner and wine director of San Francisco's A16 and SPQR.

Italian restaurants in America present a natural opportunity to help spread the bitter word on amaro. Too often, though, amaro is mixed in with grappa and limoncello and brandy on the after-dinner drinks list, and the unfamiliar names and even the word amaro may not mean much to a diner. And even when restaurants are on top of their game and have a well-represented, A-to-Z list of amari and their provenance on the menu, it can still be challenging. Knowing that Amaro Nonino Quintessentia hails from Friuli, Italy, is helpful, but some more subtle cues or buzzwords on the menu, like you might see with a wine list, to help describe its signature taste and set up an expectation of what's to come, would be even better. On the hospitality front, you could argue that that's the point of the server, to spark that conversation with the diner and help with any additional education on the topic. But more often than not, I think the A-to-Z list of amari can still look exotic and

intimidating to those unfamiliar with the category, and they're likely to pass and just stick with an espresso rather than have a nice glass of Averna.

With America's growing obsession with restaurant culture and documenting everything we eat, amaro's natural bridge to the food world still shows untapped potential. Beyond Italian restaurants, I've seen single-serving bottles of the German herbal digestif Underberg served at Qui in Austin, Texas, and Pêche, in New Orleans. At Publican in Chicago, diners who've just tackled their large-format ham chop in hay can treat their food coma with the restaurant's signature Kyle's After Pork Digestif (page 121).

It's interesting to note that as amaro appreciation is starting to spike in the United States, the tradition of amaro in Italy isn't as romantic as you might imagine for the younger generation of drinkers. "Homemade amaro in Italy and aperitif and amaro culture are on the decline," says Alex Bachman. "The younger generation loves cocktails. They love whiskey. Jack Daniel's is the number one spirit in Italy. You don't see a lot of the younger generation consuming amaro." John Troia agrees, adding, "Young people don't want to drink the stuff their parents and grandparents drank. They want to drink modern things." Taylor Parsons of République in Los Angeles adds, "We're seeing a phase shift on how people drink in general. Our parents' generation tends to drink the same drink wherever they go. Our generation and the younger generation helped pave the way for the cocktail resurgence and for ordering beverages like you might order food. We're much more seasonally minded than they were. There's a more nuanced understanding with cocktails and amaro, like you saw happen with wine."

That blurry lack or regulation and classification of amaro also applies to serving amaro. Just order an Averna at a restaurant and, unless you're asked how you'd like it, you'll encounter a spin-the-wheel approach to how it arrives at the table. It can be served neat in a grappa glass, small wineglass, tumbler, rocks glass, juice glass, or sometimes in a chilled glass or even on ice. Sometimes a twist is offered, and adding a splash of soda water isn't unheard of. Leonardo Vena of the Amaro Lucano family told me that there isn't even agreement within his own family on how to serve his family's signature Amaro Lucano. "I like it chilled—either from a cold bottle or served with one ice cube. My father drinks it neat. My grandfather likes it warm with an orange zest." Alex Bachman notes, "The last time I was in Italy, amaro service was different at every single place. Sometimes it was an ounce, sometimes it was three ounces. Sometimes it was chilled, sometimes it was room temperature. There was no standard style."

Trying different amari with a group after dinner is a great way to educate yourself on what styles you're drawn to, establishing a base for further experimentation. The ability to order flights of amari has also become more common at restaurants and bars. Take this opportunity to sample smaller pours of side-by-side fernet expressions, by region or different styles, working your way from light and citrusy to medicinal and bitter. At République, Taylor Parsons's go-to flight consists of an entry-level amaro, like Amaro Montenegro; an Alpine amaro such Amaro Bràulio; a more exotic coastal amaro like Amaro Meletti; and closing with a fernet like Fernet Lazzaroni.

Staff education at restaurants is key in perfecting how a customer reacts to amaro. Phil Walters, owner of the Bristol and Balena restaurants in Chicago, held blind tastings with his staff of every bottle of amaro legally available in the United States. "'Take 'em to the bridge,' as James Brown once said. We used this information to connect the dots and developed a bitters scale of one to ten on our menu, from lighter to the most challenging but the most exciting." On his method for amaro service at his restaurants, Walters uses a standard based on what he considers the Italian norm, neat in a glass. "But I like to give them a rope-a-dope, for lack of a better word, and serve it over a large cube with a twist. It makes it feel like a cocktail, something they're already comfortable with, and sheds the illusion of it being just a digestif." This is just one of the elements I love about amaro. Although amaro is rich with history, there's no need to be a fundamentalist about your approach in serving it. Neat, with soda water, on the rocks, in a cocktail—there is no right or wrong way to enjoy amaro.

While amazing on its own, the use of amaro in cocktails has been the best vehicle for the growing appreciation and understanding of amaro in the United States, especially as amaro makes the leap from modifier to base ingredient. "Expanding the amaro category is most important for us," says Matteo Meletti, "and bartenders are our ambassadors." Phil Walters agrees that a knowledgeable bartender is key. "Not a lot of people know what amaro is. We're here to explain and help you make the decision to try it. In the end, 5 percent might be afraid and order a martini, but others are more willing to try something different." As Americans learn to appreciate bitter, a well-crafted amaro-based cocktail can serve as the Trojan Horse to inspire people to learn more about amaro and seek it out on its own merit.

VINTAGE AMARO

In the constant quest for everything old is new again, the appreciation of vintage bottles of amaro is a subset of the current amaro scene that's offering amaro aficionados a way to experience a taste of the past. Although amaro is not always listed on the menu, restaurants like Osteria Mozza in Los Angeles and Del Posto and Maialino in New York have been stocking their bars with original mid-century bottles. At the Chicago Athletic Assocation Hotel in Chicago, there's a small coffee shop off the main lobby that at night transforms into the Milk Room, an intimate, candle-lit, eight-stool bar devoted to vintage spirits. Celebrated Chicago bartender Paul McGee opened the bar, a former speakeasy, to celebrate vintage spirits in their historic context, with drinks ranging from $28 to $100 for a Brooklyn made with vintage Amer Picon. It's always enlightening to sample vintage and contemporary spirits side by side, but sipping an Old Pal made with Campari from 1962 can serve as a relatively affordable time machine. Bars like Chicago's Billy Sunday and Canon in Seattle pride themselves on their extensive collections and have captain's lists available upon request, if you're willing to take a tour through the bittersweet decades for the right price. In January 2016, Billy Sunday's Alex Bachman launched the company Sole Agent, where he serves as a brokerage to make his portfolio of rare and vintage spirits available for wholesale distribution.

He's quick to point out that just because it's vintage doesn't mean it's going to be great. "They can oxidize or they could've had a bad bottling. Remember, we're talking about production that has no oversight. Some of these guys were doing whatever they wanted." When it comes to white whales on Bachman's punch list, he says, "Unquestionably, the most difficult amari to track down is anything pre-1948. This era is very hard to find for a number of reasons. The early 1900s saw an exodus from the brotherhoods due to anticlerical laws, and after World War II and going into the 1950s and 1960s, there was an evolution of the modern pharmaceutical industry in Italy. This was a shift from the small, local pharmacies all over Italy that had been largely responsible for producing these amari and fernet for the past one hundred and fifty or two hundred years in some cases." Francesco Amodeo, a third-generation Italian distiller from the Amalfi Coast and the creator of the made-in-America Amaro delle Sirene out of Washington, D.C., thinks contemporary amaro has gone too sweet. "The problem is, Italians have forgotten the definition of the word *amaro*. It means 'bitter.' But most amaro tends to be sweet, with some bitterness coming at the end. The medicinal amari once produced were much more bitter, but to be sold to the public they had to be sweeter to camouflage the bitterness."

You can find some vintage amari online or at specialty liquor stores, like Astor Wines and Spirits or Chambers Street Wines in New York, or if you're willing to be a bit adventurous, you can try a rare flight at a bar or restaurant specializing in amaro. Bachman says, "Anytime you get to see how these products matured over time from how they were at inception is always a really amazing experience."

AMARO IN THE WILD

In the past few years, as more amaro from Italy has become available in the United States, it's become more likely that your neighborhood bar will have a bottle or two beyond Campari and Fernet-Branca.

Taylor Parsons says, "The penetration of the category is totally different from even just a few years ago. There are early adopters, bleeding-edge people who are not mystified by strange ingredients, and then the general public who really doesn't understand amaro." Then there are bars that go out of their way to make amaro a priority in their drinks program. The following three establishments represent nirvana for amaro geeks. Beyond their inventory of bitter bottles, the common denominator in what makes them so special is their sense of hospitality and goodwill in helping demystify the sometimes confounding world of amaro. They strive to elevate their customers' understanding and appreciation of a centuries-old elixir.

AMOR Y AMARGO
New York, New York

The first bar in New York—or on the East Coast, for that matter—wholly devoted to bitters and amari opened in the East Village on March 21, 2011. Owner Ravi DeRossi, along with opening partners Avery and Janet Glasser of Bittermens and Mayur Subbarao, created a pop-up that ended up sticking around. The Glassers and Subbarao have moved on to other projects, but Sother Teague (pictured at right), who has been bartending there since the beginning and is now the bar's beverage director, told me that the bar, which means "love and bitters" in Spanish, "started as a clubhouse that we built for ourselves, but then people kept coming and leaving their money."

The 240-square-foot bar, packed with dozens upon dozens of bitters bottles and an extensive collection of bitter spirits from around the world, has a pared-down approach to service, offering only stirred drinks and no juices—the only citrus are the twists used as garnishes on some drinks. "Seltzer water is the only nonalcoholic thing I've got behind the bar and I can serve it as three versions of the same thing—flat, frozen, or bubbly," says Teague. Unlike many bars, there are no homemade syrups, shrubs, or bitters. "We don't make anything in-house. Everything we serve comes out of a bottle, and as long as that bottle is still being made, we can keep serving it to that customer who comes in asking for a drink he might've had here a year ago." Almost all of the drinks served at Amor y Amargo can be broken down into four types: the Manhattan, Negroni, old-fashioned, and Americano. There are no coupe glasses—just rocks glasses and highballs. Teague strategically places a bottle of Jägermeister in the center of his backbar to make sure there's at least one familiar bottle to those who haven't had an amaro since their college days (whether they knew it or not).

"When customers come in and say they don't like bitter, I tell them, of course you don't. You're genetically predisposed to not like bitter. It's an acquired taste. You have to tell your brain to shut up." Teague aims to break down the flavor components of his cocktails by developing a language that speaks to the universal language of food. He's also developed side projects within the bar, including the weekends-only Double Buzz, where he partners with a barista to present two kindred spirits—amaro and coffee. Japanese-style pour-over coffee is paired side by side with glasses of amaro and up to six amaro-and-coffee cocktails are featured on the menu. He's also collaborated with Lower East Side ice cream shop Luca and Bosco to develop a rotating amaro-flavored ice cream. Another ongoing series is Two Weeks Notice, where the bar is closed for the night, Amor y Amargo house rules are broken, and experimental cocktails are paired with a prix-fixe menu cooked by Teague, who once worked as a research and technical chef for Alton Brown's TV series *Good Eats*.

Teague has mastered what he calls a "lean back versus lean in" approach when it comes to explaining amaro and bitters to his customers, the better for other interested parties to hear his helpful information on the subject. "You've got to read your guests and understand their level of interest or knowledge or development on the subject. They might not recognize any of these bottles, but they'll look around and think, there's a bunch of happy people around me, so something's going right in here. There's no reason to be afraid. I sell hospitality. How much hospitality do you want? Great. That'll be fifteen dollars, please."

BILLY SUNDAY

Chicago, Illinois

Opened on January 23, 2013, Chicago bar Billy Sunday is home to the largest collection of amari in the country, with more than six hundred different bottles, including two hundred varieties of fernet, with rare bottles dating back to the early 1900s. Alex Bachman (pictured at right), a partner at Billy Sunday, oversees the curation of the extensive collection. His love of the terroir-driven aspects of wine led him to learn more about amaro, explaining, "Not to say that distilled spirits don't have a sense of place, but for me, amari really epitomizes the sense of terroir of place, whether the botanicals are locally sourced or imported to the region."

The bar's namesake, William Ashley "Billy" Sunday, was a baseball player for the Chicago White Stockings in the late 1800s but went through what Bachman politely calls "a professional transformation" and became an evangelical preacher affiliated with the temperance movement that lead up to Prohibition and the passing of the Volstead Act. "It's not without a sense of irony that you chose to name a bar for a guy who spent most his life preaching against the ills of alcohol," says Bachman.

"But however you feel about him, he was a guy who was unflinchingly committed. We had a good deal of respect for the level of conviction he had. While, of course, we are very passionate about something else, we share a similar degree of passion."

For Bachman, introducing people to the world of amaro all begins on the service side. "Our staff is heavily trained to foster an open dialogue with customers. We're custodians of these products. We need to have humility and not be grandiose to make people feel welcome." Bachman and his staff also host a regularly sold-out "Amaro, I Love You" series, where a limited number of guests are led through tastings of up to twenty rare bottles of amaro through the decades, including Cynar from the 1950s and pre-World War II fernet.

"I continue to be surprised at the bar at the number of people who give us a small little window of 'it doesn't bother me too much' when we ask how they feel about bitter. Truthfully, most don't come out and say, 'I love it.' In reality, the majority of amaro isn't necessarily that bitter. We can always find something that suits you."

BARNACLE
Seattle, Washington

When the crowds at Renee Erickson's Ballard restaurant the Walrus and the Carpenter were consistently facing a two- to four-hour wait for a seat, she began to wonder about the possibility of opening a satellite bar. Her wish came true when she bought the former bicycle repair shop next door and opened Barnacle, her version of a Seattle aperitivo bar, on September 18, 2013. The bar focuses on amaro and vermouth from Italy but with elements from Spanish and French wine bars. It was first envisioned as a place where people could pass the time waiting for their name to come up on the wait list, but has become a destination unto itself. The narrow 755-square-foot annex stocks two hundred bottles of old-world aperitifs and digestifs, with more than forty bottles of amaro and thirty bottles of vermouth. Barnacle co-owner and operator David Little (pictured at right) told me that Erickson was influenced by *Charlie and the Chocolate Factory* and wanted Barnacle to look like a "grown-up candy shop."

As with Amor y Amargo, there's no juice or egg whites or shaken drinks and just one bottle each of gin, rye, and vodka. Little points out that, especially in Seattle, there was resentment among customers regarding the pre-Prohibition-era cocktail fad. "There can sometimes be a certain level of condescension across the bar, and the whole bow ties, suspenders, and handlebar mustaches thing is fun, but makes it pretty hard to be accessible." Instead, Little and his team greet their customers with what he calls "an air of humility and empathy" to make the "esoteric old world of amaro accessible." He helps spread his philosophy with a phrase he often writes on customers' checks: *Ciao! Be Kind. Drink Bitter.*

CHAPTER 2

EXPLORING THE WORLD OF
AMARO

APERITIVO BITTERS

Aperitivo bitters use many of the same ingredients and production methods as amaro, but the color of these bitters is the first thing that sets them apart from amaro. Aperitivo bitters are typically bright orange or red and are traditionally consumed before dinner as an aperitif. Typically lighter and lower in alcohol than amaro (though some amaro is equally low in proof), they're rarely drunk on their own but instead mixed with soda or sparkling wine.

I was corrected many times by Italians who assured me with the utmost certainty that Campari is not an amaro, but a bitter. "No, no, no, absolutely not," said Matteo Meletti when I pressed him on the issue. In Italy there's universal agreement that rather than the ingredients that make up an amaro, the true definition of the word is guided by the act of when you drink it—at the end of a meal. Amaro maker Francesco Amodeo, owner of Washington D.C.'s Don Ciccio and Figli, grew up on Italy's Amalfi Coast, and he, too, is opinionated on the topic. "People should categorize things: these are aperitivos, these are digestivos. It's all about the color. If it's red, drink it before; if it's dark, drink it after. An aperitivo should have the color of the sunset. At nighttime when it's dark, you want an amaro to digest."

To make it even more confusing, even though *amaro* is Italian for "bitter," Italians will use the English word *bitter* to describe the categories of both aperitivo bitters and cocktail bitters like Angostura and Peychaud's. Katie Parla, author of *Tasting Rome: Fresh Flavors and Forgotten Recipes from an Ancient City*, assures me, "You are never going to get universal agreement on the subject because Italians use all sorts of nomenclature, depending on the region and application of a liqueur. Linguistic confusion abounds."

In most American bars and liquor stores, Campari is shelved shoulder to shoulder with bottles of amaro, and many American bartenders call Campari and Aperol and their sunset-hued brothers and sisters amaro without any hesitation. As Sother Teague, of New York City's beloved bitters bar Amor y Amargo, pointed out, similar ingredients are used to make both aperitif and digestif bitters. "Campari is absolutely an amaro. This blurriness is so detrimental to the category as a whole. Amari can be both aperitif and digestif—the functionality is the same." Noted bitters and amaro authority Avery Glasser of Bittermens Spirits and DALA Spirits agrees: "An aperitivo versus a digestif is mostly psychological. Things that are drier and have more citrus can be better as an aperitif. Something sweeter with more burnt caramel can be better as a digestif."

All of the following aperitivo bitters are available for purchase in the United States, with varying degrees of ease or difficulty depending on where you live.

CAMPARI

Milan, Lombardy, Italy

ALCOHOL BY VOLUME
24 percent

NOTES
*Ruby red in color.
Bright bitter orange
rounded with light
floral notes and herbal
woodiness.*

The recipes of most amari are proprietary and passed down from generation to generation, but many producers will often share a key ingredient or two with the general public. But the ingredients of Campari, one of the world's most famous amari, remain a closely guarded secret, with the only two known ingredients being alcohol and water. Beyond that, the recipe is based on an "infusion of herbs, aromatic plants, and fruit in alcohol and water." I pressed the Gruppo Campari public relations executive for more during my private tour of Galleria Campari in Sesto San Giovanni, on the grounds of Campari's first commercial production facility. "There's obviously orange or chinotto. And gentian, right?" But my query was met with a polite smile and repeated mention of alcohol and water being the only publicly shared ingredients of the more than 150-year-old secret recipe.

Campari is distributed to more than 180 countries and more than three million cases are sold annually, but it started out in 1860 when Gaspare Campari created his signature formula, then called Bitter all'Uso d'Holanda, in Novara, Italy. In 1867, he opened Caffè Campari in Milan's prestigious Piazza del Duomo, where the drink caught on as an aperitif. His sons Davide and Guido took over the company in 1904, building the Sesto San Giovanni production facility at a location with key access to railway hubs to help spread their brand across Italy and beyond. Traditionally served on the rocks with a splash of soda, Campari became a key ingredient in the Americano (page 90) and Negroni (page 107) and has been adapted by bartenders to become a versatile component in contemporary cocktails.

In the early and mid-twentieth century, notable artists like Ugo Mochi partnered with the brand, helping to spread the word of Campari through graphic illustrations and paintings that became a key in their advertising outreach. In 1985, Frederico Fellini even directed an Italian television commercial for Campari, and today Campari's pop culture partnership continues with international commercial campaigns that have featured actresses Salma Hayek and Jessica Alba, along with an annual Campari calendar that has spotlighted Uma Thurman and Eva Green, among others.

While the secret recipe is said to have remain unchanged, there was one alteration to the source of that trademark Campari red color. Until 2006, Campari was colored with carmine, a dye made from crushed, dried cochineal insects. The ruby hue now comes from a synthetic red dye.

In addition to Campari, Gruppo Campari's Italian portfolio includes the amaro brands Aperol, Averna, Bràulio, and Cynar.

APEROL

Milan, Lombardy, Italy

ALCOHOL BY VOLUME
11 percent

KNOWN INGREDIENTS
Bitter and sweet oranges, gentian, rhubarb

NOTES
Bright sunset orange in color. Fresh orange sweetness with very light bitterness.

Aperol launched in 1919, when the brothers Silvio and Luigi Barbieri debuted their low-alcohol, bright orange-hued aperitivo bitter made from thirty herbs, spices, and fruit. Aperol's awareness grew after World War II through advertising in bars and cafés that served it, and it attracted a younger crowd of social drinkers, especially women. The "Ah, Aperol!" advertisements from the 1970s starring Italian actor Tino Buazzelli aired during the *Il Carosello* program throughout Italy, helping launch a catchphrase and further brand recognition. And Aperol has long been associated with its most popular delivery method, the Aperol Spritz (page 93). Since 2005, global advertising campaigns for the Aperol spritz have helped it become one of the most ubiquitous drinks across Italy and beyond.

The formula for Aperol has remained unchanged since its inception, but it is now produced by Gruppo Campari, which acquired the brand in 2003. It was first imported to the United States in 2006.

CAPPELLETTI VINO APERITIVO AMERICANO ROSSO

Aldeno, Trentino-Alto Adige, Italy

ALCOHOL BY VOLUME
17 percent

KNOWN INGREDIENTS
Gentian, orange peel

NOTES
Candy apple red. Lightly sweet with hint of citrus peel bitterness.

Hailing from Trentino-Alto Adige in Northern Italy, this bright-red, wine-based aperitivo is made from a base of mostly Trebbiano grapes, bittersweet citrus, and herbs and has been made by the same family for four generations. Its crimson color comes from cochineal, a natural red dye made from the crushed carapace of South American beetles. It has the versatility of a vermouth and is sort of a bridge between Aperol and Campari. Excellent when used in a spritz (page 93).

CASONI 1814 APERITIVO

Modena, Emilia-Romagna, Italy

ALCOHOL BY VOLUME
15 percent

NOTES
Pale red. Lightly floral. Herbal with bittersweet notes of grapefruit and candied orange peel.

Made to celebrate the birth of the artisanal distillery founded by Giuseppe Casoni in Finale Emilia in Emilia-Romagna in 1814, this blend of "local herbs, fruits, and seeds" is an excellent, aromatic, lightly bitter liqueur that's perfect for aperitif cocktails such as the Cardinal (page 136). Mario Casoni represents the sixth generation of the family business.

CONTRATTO APERITIF

Canelli, Piedmont, Italy

Founded in Canelli, Italy, in 1867 by Giuseppe Contratto, Contratto is the oldest continuously operating producer of sparkling wine in Italy. In 1993, the winery was sold to the nearby Bocchino grappa distillery, and in June 2011, the winery La Spinetta acquired the company. Along with introducing three new vermouths and a fernet (see page 52), Contratto has revisited archival recipes for two aperitivo releases that hit shelves in summer 2015, called Contratto Aperitif and Contratto Bitter. Contratto Aperitif, which, like Aperol, is best put to use in a spritz (page 93) or low-alcohol cocktail, features twenty-eight ingredients and is based on a 1935 recipe.

ALCOHOL BY VOLUME
13.5 percent

KNOWN INGREDIENTS
Aloe, angelica root, bitter orange, cardamom, cascarilla, cinchona bark, cloves, ginger, hawthorn, juniper berries, lemon peel, licorice, nettle, rhubarb, safflower, sage, sweet orange, tangerine peel, wormwood

NOTES
Bright orange. Sweet and bitter oranges with light herbal and woody bitterness.

CONTRATTO BITTER

Canelli, Piedmont, Italy

Contratto Bitter, formulated from a 1933 recipe, is best put to work as a cocktail mixer, subbing in where you might use Campari. Both the Contratto Bitter and the Aperitif are all-natural blends of herbs, spices, fruit, and seeds infused in Italian brandy, with their bright red and orange coloring coming from carrot and beet extracts.

ALCOHOL BY VOLUME
22 percent

KNOWN INGREDIENTS
Bitter orange peel, cardamom, cloves, inula (horse-heal), gentian, ginger, hibiscus, juniper berries, mint, nettle, rhubarb, sage, sweet orange peel

NOTES
Rich, ruby red. Sweet and bitter with subtle citrus notes and a hint of vanilla.

LUXARDO APERITIVO

Padua, Veneto, Italy

The family-owned Luxardo Distillery was founded in Torreglia, Italy, in the province of Padua in 1947 after Giorgio Luxardo, the only member of his immediate family to survive World War II, left his home of Zara (now a part of Croatia) with a cherry sapling from the orchard at his family's distillery, which had been founded in 1821. Today the fifth and sixth generations of the Luxardo family oversee operations of their world-famous Italian liqueurs and cocktail cherries. In addition to the Aperitivo and Bitter, they also produce an amaro (see page 39) and a fernet (see page 55).

ALCOHOL BY VOLUME
11 percent

KNOWN INGREDIENTS
Citrus, gentian, rhubarb

NOTES
Bright orange. Jolly Rancher strawberry candy with sweet orange fruitiness and lightly bitter aftertaste.

LUXARDO BITTER

Padua, Veneto, Italy

ALCOHOL BY VOLUME
25 percent

KNOWN INGREDIENTS
Bitter orange, marjoram, mint, sweet orange, rhubarb root, thyme

NOTES
Cherry red. Sweet and bitter with notes of freshly zested orange and dried citrus.

First made in 1885, the Luxardo Bitter is a classic aperitivo-style infusion of citrus, herbs, and spices. Best served on the rocks, with a sparkling wine or soda water, or in a Negroni as a Campari substitute.

MELETTI 1870 BITTER

Ascoli Piceno, Marche, Italy

ALCOHOL BY VOLUME
25 percent

KNOWN INGREDIENTS
Bitter orange, cinnamon, clove, coriander, gentian, sweet orange

NOTES
Bright crimson. Fruity bubble gum with anise notes. Balance of sweet and spice with mild bitterness.

Introduced in the winter of 2015, the newest bottle in Meletti's extensive portfolio of amaro, anisette, and cordials is named for the year they were founded in Ascoli Picino, in the Marche region of Italy. The mix is a blend of three separate distillates of sweet orange, bitter orange, and an infusion of herbs, spices, and botanicals. Try it sipped straight on the rocks, with a splash of soda, or subbed in for your next Americano or Negroni.

GRAN CLASSICO BITTER

Kallnach, Bern, Switzerland

ALCOHOL BY VOLUME
28 percent

KNOWN INGREDIENTS
Bitter orange, gentian, hyssop, rhubarb, wormwood

NOTES
Burnt amber. Highly aromatic with a bitter orange peel, rhubarb, and floral note rounded out with bitterness from the wormwood.

Unlike most of the red-colored aperitivo bitters, Gran Classico is made without any artificial color or flavors from a maceration of twenty-five roots and herbs and botanicals following a recipe from the 1860s based on the Italian Bitter of Turin, the model of bitters that Campari would make famous around the world. In 1925, the Swiss distillery E. Luginbühl purchased the recipe and sold it locally until California's Tempus Fugit Spirits began importing it to the United States in 2010. Tempus Fugit's John Troia is quite enamored with the natural amber color of Gran Classico: "Why Campari dyed it red when you can get a color like this, I'll never know."

LEOPOLD BROS. APERITIVO

Denver, Colorado, United States

It shouldn't come as any surprise that America's first foray into the classic aperitivo-style bitter comes from experimental small-batch distiller Todd Leopold, who has been creating his distinctly American take on classic European spirits—including a fernet (see page 58)—from his distillery in Denver, Colorado. He created a limited run of the aperitivo in 2013 to celebrate his wedding, but the final version was released in summer 2015, just in time for Negroni Week, the worldwide charity event held each June that celebrates bartender and cocktail afficiandos' renewed passion for this bittersweet superstar of the cocktail world. The Leopold vodka is the base spirit, which is infused with grapefruit peel, gentian, and even sarsaparilla in a nod to that American classic, root beer. The vibrant red color comes from all-natural cochineal.

ALCOHOL BY VOLUME
24 percent

KNOWN INGREDIENTS
Artemisia pontica, coriander, gentian, grapefruit peel, hyssop, sarsaparilla root, vanilla, wormwood

NOTES
Bright red. Bitter, sweet, and floral with earthy, dry depth.

PEYCHAUD'S APERITIVO

Frankfort, Kentucky, United States

Released in 2015 from Peychaud's, whose iconic cocktail bitters have been spiking classic New Orleans cocktails since the 1830s, this bottle represents their debut into the aperitivo category.

ALCOHOL BY VOLUME
11 percent

NOTES
Cherry cough syrup red. Lightly bitter and aromatic with anise notes.

AMARO

If you visit Italy and you're an amaro aficionado, you will be overwhelmed by the sheer number of bottles, brands, and special blends you'll encounter. Booze nerds will often e-mail me and ask what bottles they should smuggle back (always claim your spirits!) in their suitcase. Each year, more Italian brands are becoming available in the United States, but there are still many suitcases' worth of space to fill up. I like to bring back something I can't get in the States, ideally with origins from where I've visited, like a bottle of Amaro San Simone from Piedmont, named after the brotherhood of sixteenth-century monks from Turin. Once it's back home on your bar, twisting off the cap and pouring a glass can have a transformative effect. There are hundreds of amari available in Italy, from larger commercial brands to small-batch producers to home brew served at restaurants. This lineup of made-in-Italy amaro is a survey of bottles that can be found for sale in the United States, with varying degrees of ease or difficulty depending on where you live.

AMARA AMARO D'ARANCIA ROSSA

Paternò, Sicily, Italy

ALCOHOL BY VOLUME
30 percent

KNOWN INGREDIENTS
Bitter orange peel

NOTES
Amber color. Dominant sweet citrus notes with light spice. Minimal bitterness.

This contemporary amaro developed in 2014 by Rossa founders Giuseppe Librizzi and Edward Strange makes the most of the bounty of Sicilian blood oranges and can almost be used in place of triple sec in cocktails. Two different varieties of blood oranges, Gallo Tarot and Tarot Nocellara, are infused with herbs for a limited production of fifteen thousand bottles annually. Available on the shelves at Eataly outposts, select liquor stores, and Italian restaurants in the United States.

AVERNA

Caltanissetta, Sicily, Italy

ALCOHOL BY VOLUME
29 percent

KNOWN INGREDIENTS
Lemon and orange essential oils, pomegranate

NOTES
Deep rusty brown. Notes of cola, orange peel, licorice, and vanilla. Sweet with soft and subtle bitterness.

While Averna began in 1868, the recipe for what would be become Amaro Averna dates back to the Benedictine monks of the San Spirito Abbey in Caltanissetta, Sicily, who had been using the formula as an herbal elixir well before then. This spirited connection happened in 1859, when the monks passed along the secret formula to Sicilian businessman Salvatore Averna, who was a benefactor of the abbey, as a token of their gratitude. What started out as a spirit with local appeal grew in scale when by 1895 Salvatore's son Francesco presented Averna at fairs and expos across Italy and abroad. By 1912, Averna was the official supplier to the royal house of King Vittorio Emanuele III and the royal coat of arms was permitted to be displayed on the label of the bottle. After Francesco's untimely death, his wife, Anna Marie, ran the company until their children, Salvatore, Paolo, Emilio, and Michelle, took the helm, helping expand Averna's reach even farther, including to the United States. In 1958, the Fratelli Averna corporation was founded and Averna went on to become one of the most well-known and best-selling amari from Italy. Its medium-bodied profile with a well-balanced blend of lightly bitter and sweet has made it a favorite among bartenders for its versatility in contemporary, amaro-centric cocktails like the Black Manhattan (page 127). After five generations of family ownership, Fratelli Averna (along with their portfolio, which includes Amaro Bràulio) was acquired by Gruppo Campari in 2014 for $143 million dollars. The storage of the botanicals and herbal infusion for Averna still takes place in Caltanissetta, Sicily, but all Gruppo Campari products are then manufactured, bottled, and distributed from their factory outside of Milan.

AMARO BRÀULIO

Valtellina, Lombardy, Italy

Born in Bormio, Valtellina, in the Italian Alps near the Swiss border, this ultimate après-ski amaro was created by a chemist named Dr. Francesco Peloni in 1875 and features a host of secret Alpine herbs and botanicals that were traditionally foraged from the Bormio hillsides. Aged for two years in Slavonian oak barrels, it's an amaro whose provenance is apparent with each sip. Amaro Bràulio became a darling among amaro geeks when it was first imported to the United States in 2013, and its limited availability after Gruppo Campari purchased the brand in 2014 has made it even more in demand. While they're not available in the United States, the annual limited bottlings of Amaro Bràulio Riserva Speciale Millesimata—made in smaller barrels and with a higher proof (24.7 percent alcohol)—are worth seeking out when traveling in Europe.

ALCOHOL BY VOLUME
21 percent

KNOWN INGREDIENTS
Gentian, juniper, wormwood, yarrow

NOTES
Dark brown color. Highly aromatic with pine, spearmint, and chamomile, with notes of floral bitterness and warm spice.

CAPPELLETTI ELISIR NOVASALUS VINO AMARO

Aldeno, Trentino-Alto Adige, Italy

Based on a recipe from the 1920s and first imported into the United States in 2014, the dry Marsala wine–based Elisir Novasalus is made through a six-month-long maceration of Alpine herbs and flowers and unique ingredients like Sicilian tree sap. It's a tough one to mix into cocktails and on its own it's bold and complex, with severe layers of bitterness and not a hint of sweetness. If you're tasting through a flight of amari, you'll want to save this guy for last.

ALCOHOL BY VOLUME
16 percent

KNOWN INGREDIENTS
Aloe, burdock, cinchona bark, dandelion, gentian, tree sap

NOTES
Mahogany color. Extremely bold, dry, and bracingly bitter.

CARDAMARO VINO AMARO

Canelli, Piedmont, Italy

Since 1820, seven generations of the Bosca family have been making wine in Piedmont, Italy. Formulated more than one hundred years ago, their Cardamaro Vino Amaro uses Piedmontese Moscato as a base for an infusion of herbs and botanicals, including cardoon (a relative of the artichoke) and blessed thistle. It's aged for six months in new oak barrels. A lighter amaro, it is best used it in place of vermouth or sherry in a cocktail.

ALCOHOL BY VOLUME
17 percent

KNOWN INGREDIENTS
Blessed thistle, cardoon

NOTES
Light caramel color. Sweet herbal bitterness rounded with orange peel and pine.

AMARO CIOCIARO

Frosinone, Lazio, Italy

ALCOHOL BY VOLUME
30 percent

NOTES
Dark brown color. Earthy with mild bitterness. Notes of sweet and bitter orange and dark chocolate.

Named after its region of origin in central Italy, Amaro CioCiaro has been produced since 1873, when Vincenzo Paolucci moved from Abruzzo to Sora in Ciociaria. His son Donato joined the family enterprise after World War I, but World War II disrupted business and the factory was heavily damaged. After World War II, Donato's sons, Mario and Ermanno, rebuilt the production facility and spread awareness of the brand through marketing and advertising efforts in Italy. Today, the fourth generation of the Paolucci family keeps the formula a closely guarded secret, revealing only that their amaro is made up of alcohol, caramelized sugar, and natural herbs. But it's a safe bet that gentian and bitter and sweet orange peels are part of the blend. Cocktail historian and author David Wondrich has recommended Amaro CioCiaro as a substitute for Amer Picon, the bittersweet orange liqueur from France (often called for in classic cocktails), which isn't available in the United States.

CYNAR

Milan, Lombardy, Italy

ALCOHOL BY VOLUME
16.5 percent

KNOWN INGREDIENTS
Artichoke

NOTES
Dark brown. Savory herbal and earthy vegetal notes with sweet caramel finish.

Part of Gruppo Campari's Italian portfolio, the low-alcohol amaro emblazoned with an artichoke on its vibrant label contains thirteen different plants and herbs and takes its name from the Latin for artichoke: *Cynara scolymus*. In name and looks it would seem to have a very vegetal taste, but artichoke is just one ingredient in this cocktail-friendly amaro. Despite its murky appearance, it has a low-proof status that makes it flexible as an aperitif mixed with soda and adorned with an orange slice, or on its own as a digestif at the end of a meal. This carciofo-style amaro, the name used for artichoke-based amari, was created in 1952 by Venetian philanthropist Angelo Dalle Molle. It grew in popularity in the 1960s perhaps in part due to television ads starring actor Ernesto Calindri that had the tagline "Cynar, against the strain of modern life."

In the summer of 2015, Cynar 70 Proof came to market, doubling the amount of alcohol in the original recipe. This bold new bitter is perfect for the bar industry crowd, who tend to take their amaro in shot form.

AMARO D'ERBE NINA

Carpesica, Veneto, Italy

Sisters-in-law Cinzia Canzian and Pier Francesca Bonicelli have been making artisanal sparkling wine in the Veneto region of Conegliano and Valdobbiadene since 2004. In 2015, they added the Alpine-style Amaro d'Erbe to their portfolio, based on a recipe of thirty local herbs from Canzian's Aunt Nina. Best served chilled or with an ice cube.

ALCOHOL BY VOLUME
30 percent

KNOWN INGREDIENTS
Fennel, gentian, mint, orange peel

NOTES
Lightly sweet with flavors of mint and orange among balanced Alpine bitterness.

AMARO DELL'ERBORISTA

Muccia, Marche, Italy

Founded in 1868 on the slopes of the Sibillini Mountains in Italy's Marche region by noted herbalist Girolamo Varnelli, the Varnelli distillery makes two of the finest examples of craft-made amari with their Amaro Dell'Erborista and Amaro Sibilla. One of the signature styles of Varnelli amari is the process of decoction, where the herbs, roots, and spices are fire-roasted before the maceration process. Varnelli CEO Orietta Maria Varnelli, one of the quartet of female heirs from the fourth generation running the family business, explained that compared to a controlled flame, the imperfections of using a natural fire is just another element of what makes their all-natural products unique. The final touch is using local, multi-flower raw Sibillian honey as a sweetener.

The flip-capped bottle of the Amaro Dell'Erborista (the herbalist's amaro), created in the mid-1980s based on a historical family recipe, is aged for at least seven months and left unfiltered, resulting in a distinctive cloudy appearance with bits of sediment.

ALCOHOL BY VOLUME
21 percent

KNOWN INGREDIENTS
Bitter orange peel, cinchona bark, cinnamon, clove, gentian, honey, rhubarb root

NOTES
Tobacco brown. Smoky and very dry with presence of sandalwood, spicy fruit, and honey.

FORO AMARO SPECIALE

Piedmont, Italy

First available in the United States in 2014, this blend of twenty-five different botanicals is a milder, gateway amaro that is delicious on its own and also very cocktail-friendly—use it like you would Averna.

ALCOHOL BY VOLUME
30 percent

KNOWN INGREDIENTS
Angelica root, gentian, hibiscus, lemon peel, marjoram, orange peel, sage

NOTES
Dark brown color. Blend of herbs, citrus, and chocolate.

AMARO LAZZARONI

Saronno, Lombardy, Italy

ALCOHOL BY VOLUME
25 percent

NOTES
Amber. Herbal bitterness with notes of burnt sugar and peppermint.

The red banner and mountain landscape on the label of this bottle might remind you of Amaro Bràulio, and both brands take advantage of aromatic Alpine herbs as primary ingredients. Founded in 1851, Paolo Lazzaroni e Figli remains family owned and is famous for its colorful tins of Lazzaroni amaretti cookies.

LORENZO INGA MY AMARO

Gavi, Piedmont, Italy

ALCOHOL BY VOLUME
30 percent

NOTES
Sweet and mild with bitter orange and menthol notes.

Created by award-winning grappa makers, who started their family business in Noto, Sicily, in 1832, My Amaro (sold as Mio Amaro in Italy) is based on a blend of more than thirty different herbs, barks, and roots that's then aged for two months.

AMARO LUCANO

Pisticci Scalo, Basilicata, Italy

ALCOHOL BY VOLUME
28 percent

KNOWN INGREDIENTS
Aloe ferox, angelica root, bitter orange, blessed thistle, elderberry, gentian, musk yarrow, rue, sage, wormwood

NOTES
Mahogany color. Medium sweetness with herbal bitterness and notes of cinnamon, licorice, and caramel.

Headquartered in Pisticci Scalo, a small southern Italian town in the Matera provice in the region of Basilicata, the Lucano brand was founded in 1894 by Cavalier Pasquale Vena, and his descendants, now representing the fourth generation, run the family business to this day. The name *Lucano* originates from Lucania, the ancient Latin name for the Basilicata region. Cavaliere Vena got his start as a baker, and by 1900, he and the amaro that he had started making in the back room of his bakery were the official supplier to the House of Savoy and known all across Italy. Production ramped up until World War II brought a halt to operations, but by the 1960s a new factory was built and in the 1980s advertisements with the slogan "What do you want from life? A Lucano" kept brand awareness on the upswing.

Fifth-generation Pasquale Vena holds the formula to the family amaro close, as his sons, Leonardo and Francesco, and daughter Letizia, help take their brand to a new generation of cocktail enthusiasts. It includes a blend of more than thirty herbs and spices, many of which are shared in detail on the Lucano website and promotional materials. As with Fernet-Branca, knowing the ingredients will only get you so far. It's all about mastering the ratios and balancing the blends during production. In 2015, the family released a full-bodied, higher-proof (34 percent alcohol by volume) Anniversario edition of Amaro Lucano to mark the 120th anniversary of its founding.

LUXARDO AMARO ABANO

Padua, Veneto, Italy

Named after the Roman spa town in Veneto famous for its hot springs and mud baths, Amaro Abano was created in 1952 using wild, local herbs and botanicals sourced from the Euganean Hills near the Luxardo distillery.

ALCOHOL BY VOLUME
30 percent

KNOWN INGREDIENTS
Bitter orange peel, cardamom, cinchona bark, cinnamon, condurango

NOTES
Dark brown. Herbaceous notes of orange peel, mint, black pepper, and baking spices with a middle-of-the-road, even bitterness.

AMARO MELETTI

Ascoli Piceno, Marche, Italy

In 1871 in Ascoli Piceno, in the Marche region of Italy, Silvio Meletti perfected a cold-extraction process known as percolation to create his namesake anisette, the classic sweet, licorice-tasting spirit made using locally harvested anise seeds, that would go on to win countless awards and became a known entity behind bars across Italy and the entire world. Now in its fifth generation as a family-owned business, Meletti introduced an amaro, among the anisette, cordials, and liqueurs, in the early twentieth century. Based on formulas from founder Silvio's recipe books and later perfected by fourth-generation owner Silvio Meletti—the father of Matteo and Mauro Meletti, who represent the family's fifth generation—Amaro Meletti sources many ingredients, including its signature saffron, from within the Marche region of Italy. It's one of the most affordable amari on the market and one of the favorites among early amaro aficionados. Matteo admits that they may have underpriced themselves when they entered the market, but it also means that bartenders, keeping an eye on the bottom line, will likely reach for Meletti as a modifier or base in amaro-spiked cocktails. (See "Tasting History in Ascoli Piceno," page 41.)

ALCOHOL BY VOLUME
32 percent

KNOWN INGREDIENTS
Anise, clove, gentian, orange peel, saffron, violet flower

NOTES
Light amber color. Floral notes with cinnamon, saffron, and gingerbread spice.

AMARO MONTENEGRO

Bologna, Emilia-Romagna, Italy

ALCOHOL BY VOLUME
23 percent

KNOWN INGREDIENTS
Orange peel, vanilla

NOTES
Copper color. Sweet and mild with light bitterness. Notes of tangerine, cucumber, orange peel, and black cherry.

One of the best-selling amaros across Italy, Amaro Montenegro was created in 1885, a year before Coca-Cola made its debut in America. Rather than pursue a life in the clergy as originally planned, Stanislao Cobianchi instead used his knowledge of herbs gained from traveling to create a liqueur company in Bologna, eventually naming his amaro Montenegro in tribute to Princess Elena of Montenegro, who married Vittorio Emanuele III in 1896 and became Italy's second queen, reigning from 1900 to 1946. Hailed as "the liqueur of the virtues" by famed Italian poet and writer Gabriele D'Annunzio, Amaro Montenegro is comprised of a blend of forty proprietary ingredients—the complete recipe and production process are known to only three people in the company. As with many amaro companies, World War II affected production. The Montenegro factory was heavily bombed in 1941 but reopened in 1946. A fixture of advertising campaigns touting *sapore vero* (genuine flavor), Amaro Montenegro, along with Fernet-Branca, is one of the most ubiquitous bottles of amaro behind the bar. With its lighter, sweeter flavor profile, it's a popular amaro among bartenders when introducing amaro into cocktails.

AMARO NARDINI

Muccia, Veneto, Italy

ALCOHOL BY VOLUME
31 percent

KNOWN INGREDIENTS
Bitter orange, gentian, peppermint

NOTES
Brown color. Floral with notes of bitter orange, mint, and licorice.

The grappa distillery founded by Bartolo Nardini in Bassano in 1779 remains the oldest distillery in Italy. Amaro Nardini uses its famous grappa as a base with an infusion of fewer ingredients than most amari—just gentian, bitter orange, and peppermint. The distillery also offers a fernet, Elixir China, and two aperitivo bitters, Bitter and Rosso, though they're not currently available in the United States.

TASTING HISTORY IN ASCOLI PICENO

Many Italian amaro producers are still a family affair, and when I visited Ascoli Piceno in the Marche region of Italy, I was fortunate enough to spend the day with the Meletti family, whose name graces the bottles of their legendary anisette, liqueurs, and amaro. Matteo Meletti (pictured above), who with his brother, Mauro, represents the fifth generation of the family, invited me to visit the distillery, one of the oldest in Italy, and offered to be my host for the day. One of the highlights of the visit was when Matteo, Mauro, and their father, Silvio, showed me into the lab next to their offices and produced a test batch of an amaro recipe based on a formula procured from Matteo's great-great-grandfather's recipe book, which was resting on the table between us. They had already done one in-house test run to taste it, but in honor of my visit, Matteo explained that he wanted me to be the first non-family member to try it. The old-world characteristics really stood out—it was much more medicinal and bitter than the existing Amaro Meletti. "It needs to be even more bitter, no?" Matteo suggested, after taking a sip. "It's close, but not quite there." When I last saw Matteo in New York he was carrying around an unmarked bottle of the old-world Meletti blend for bartenders to sample. Hopefully, in the near future, there will be another Meletti amaro expression consumers will be able to sample on their own, but I will always cherish being able to witness its debut in Ascoli Piceno.

AMARO NONINO QUINTESSENTIA

Percoto, Friuli, Italy

ALCOHOL BY VOLUME
35 percent

KNOWN INGREDIENTS
Bitter orange peel, cinchona bark, galangal, gentian, licorice, quassia, rhubarb root, saffron, tamarind

NOTES
Amber color. Subtle herbal bitterness and gentle spice with primary notes of orange peel and caramel sweetness.

From the design of the label and bottle to the contents within, Amaro Nonino Quintessentia is one of most elegant expressions of amaro around. Known worldwide for their award-winning grappa from Friuli, the Nonino family is a true family business; Benito (pictured at right) and Giannola actively run operations with their daughters, Antonella, Cristina, and Elisabetta. Their amaro story begins in 1933, when Benito's father, Antonio Nonino, made a grappa-based amaro he called Amaro Carnia, named after the nearby mountains. In 1984, Benito and Giannola developed their proprietary ÙE Grape Distillate, a unique distillation of the whole grape—skins, pulp, and juice—that captures the production elements of a wine distillate with the craft of grappa. In 1987, reformulating the family amaro recipe using a base comprised of the ÙE and grappa distillate, the amaro was then aged for five years in barriques from Nevers and Limousin, as well as former sherry barrels, making its debut in 1992. (See "Meet the Noninos," page 44.)

AMARO RAMAZZOTTI

Canelli, Piedmont, Italy

ALCOHOL BY VOLUME
30 percent

KNOWN INGREDIENTS
Bitter orange, cardamom, clove, galangal, myrrh, star anise, sweet orange

NOTES
Cola color. Notes of root beer, orange peel, cinnamon, and aromatic, herbal bitterness.

One of the oldest commercial amari available, Amaro Ramazzotti was created in Milan in 1815 by Ausano Ramazzotti and celebrated its bicentennial in 2015. The proprietary blend of thirty-three different fruits, herbs, and botanicals rose to prominence three decades later through Café Ramazzotti, which Ausano opened in 1848 near the La Scala opera house and was famous for selling Ramazzotti in place of coffee ("we've secretly replaced their regular coffee with Ramazzotti . . ."). The Milan production facility was destroyed in World War II but was rebuilt in 1959. The company was later acquired by Pernod Ricard in 1985 and is now produced in Canelli in Piedmont. Under their label, Ramazzotti also makes an aperitivo, an aperitivo rosa, a menta, and a sambuca. I've seen the sambuca in the wild but at the time of writing the other bottlings are not yet available in the United States.

MEET THE NONINOS

In 2012, I had an article on amaro in *Bon Appétit* that included a full-page photograph of a bottle of Amaro Nonino Quintessentia. After the story ran, I received a very kind, handwritten letter from Elisabetta Nonino, who with her sisters and mother and father, runs the Nonino family business in Friuli, Italy. Since that introduction, I've had the pleasure of meeting Elisabetta (pictured above left) in person whenever she's in New York during her travels throughout the United States. Both times we've met at Maialino for a personal tasting of her family's grappa and amaro, and that's where I learned that her preferred way to drink their namesake amaro is in a small glass with two ice cubes and an orange slice. I quickly adopted this method as well and never fail to refer to it as "Elisabetta style" when I order. When I had the chance to finally visit the Noninos in Italy, I found out, in true O. Henry fashion, that Elisabetta and her mother, Giannola, would be in New York when I was in Friuli. Naturally, her sisters Antonella and Cristina were excellent hosts, and in her absence, we drank a round of their amaro Elisabetta style before lunch and had a toast in her honor.

AMARO DI SANTA MARIA AL MONTE

Genoa, Liguria, Italy

Although it does not have the word *fernet* in the name, this thirty-six all-natural ingredient amaro has common fernet ingredients, like aloe ferox, myrrh, and saffron, and many bartenders tend to shelve it alongside Fernet-Branca. In 1892, Nicola Vignale first produced Amaro di Santa Maria al Monte based on a recipe developed by Franciscan friars of the Santa Maria monastery near Florence.

ALCOHOL BY VOLUME
40 percent

KNOWN INGREDIENTS
Aloe ferox, angelica root, bitter orange peel, cardamom, cinchona bark, gentian, juniper, myrrh, nutmeg, rhubarb root, saffron

NOTES
Deep mahogany color. Pronounced herbal blast of ginseng, spearmint, pine, and cola with a rich, medicinal finish.

AMARO SEGESTA

Marsala, Sicily, Italy

Amaro Segesta was created in 1958 by Vito Giannone at Distillery Virtus in Marsala on the western edge of Sicily, using a highly guarded proprietary blend of more than twenty local herbs and spices. Later acquired by Distillery Bianchi, makers of grappa and Marsala wine, Amaro Segesta remains known for showcasing its birthplace of Sicily and has a similar profile as Averna.

ALCOHOL BY VOLUME
33 percent

NOTES
Brown color. Notes of bitter orange peel, licorice, and eucalyptus.

AMARO SIBILLA

Muccia, Marche, Italy

First produced in 1868 by herbalist Girolamo Varnelli and named for the legend of the Sibillini Mountains oracle, Sibilla, Amaro Sibilla went on to win gold medals in Rome in 1902 and again in 1909 at the International Exhibition in Turin. Aged for at least seven months, Sibilla and Dell'Erborista are two of the more expensive amari on the market (the Sibilla is more than $50 while the Dell'Erborista is north of $60), but they are both elegant and challenging bottles for when you're ready to further explore the range of amaro on the market.

ALCOHOL BY VOLUME
34 percent

KNOWN INGREDIENTS
Bitter orange peel, cinchona bark, cinnamon, clove, gentian flower, gentian root, honey, rhubarb root, sweet orange peel

NOTES
Dark brown. Bitter with dried fruit and forest floor notes rounded out with coffee and sweet honey.

AMARO SIBONA

Piobesi d'Alba, Piedmont, Italy

ALCOHOL BY VOLUME
28 percent

KNOWN INGREDIENTS
Anise, cinchona bark, gentian, mint, rhubarb root, sage

NOTES
Cherry cola color. Sweet with layered notes of cola, mint, and burnt orange peel.

Founded more than a century ago, Antica Distilleria Domenico Sibona is the oldest working distillery in the Piedmont region. First imported into the United States in the summer of 2014, Amaro Sibona is a maceration of thirty-four herbs, roots, and fruit in a grappa base of Malvasia and Sauvignon Blanc grapes.

AMARO DEL SOLE VITTONE

Milan, Lombardy, Italy

ALCOHOL BY VOLUME
30 percent

NOTES
Medium-bodied with delicate herbs and notes of cherry cola.

Comprised of twenty herbs and spices, this amaro, based on a nineteenth-century recipe, is fairly new to the United States, picking up distribution in 2014. It's already popping up as an ingredient on cocktail menus across the country.

AMARO TOSOLINI

Povoletto, Friuli, Italy

ALCOHOL BY VOLUME
30 percent

KNOWN INGREDIENTS
Angelica root, bitter orange, calamus, clove, gentian, ginger, lemon balm, mint, rosemary, star anise, wormwood

NOTES
Dark brown. More sweet than bitter, with orange peel and cinnamon notes.

Based on a recipe from Bepi Tosolini, who founded Tosolini in 1918, the amaro from the second and third generations of the Tosolini family continues their spirited tradition in Friuli with their line of grappa and liqueurs. A blend of fifteen herbs and botanicals macerates for four months in eau-de-vie in ash wood barrels.

VECCHIO AMARO DEL CAPO

Limbadi, Calabria, Italy

In 1915 Joseph Gruner founded a distillery in Santa Venerina, Sicily, on the slopes of Mount Etna. His sons joined the family business, and in 1965, Vecchio Amaro del Capo was created with an infusion of twenty-nine ingredients, highlighting the local herbs, flowers, fruit, and roots of Calabria, the "toe" of Italy's boot, surrounded by the Mediterranean sea. Firmly rooted in local Southern Italian tradition—as recently as the 1970s this was only available in Calabria—the amaro is traditionally served ice cold, straight from the freezer, and is mostly consumed during hot Calabrian summers. A modern plant run by the fourth generation of the family stands in Limbadi in Calabria. A limited-release, oak barrel–aged bottling of Vecchio Amaro del Capo Riserva was released in Italy in 2015 to celebrate the one hundredth anniversary of the Distillery Gruner.

ALCOHOL BY VOLUME
35 percent

KNOWN INGREDIENTS
Bitter orange, chamomile, juniper, licorice, sweet orange, tangerine

NOTES
Color of iced tea. Lightly bitter with the fragrant sweetness of ribbon candy.

ZUCCA RABARBARO AMARO

Milan, Lombardy, Italy

Created in 1845 by Ettore Zucca, this namesake amaro (officially "Rabarbaro Zucca Amaro") went on to become a fixture of Milanese café society, especially through its exposure as an aperitif at Caffè Zucca in Galleria across from the historic Piazza del Duomo, a frequent haunt of noted musicians like Toscanini and Verdi. A favorite elixir of King Vittorio Emanuele II, Zucca was heralded as a "Supplier of the Italian Royal House." *Zucca* means "squash" in Italian, but the other half of the more formal title for this amaro, *rabarbaro*, denotes one of the key ingredients—rhubarb root.

ALCOHOL BY VOLUME
30 percent

KNOWN INGREDIENTS
Cardamom, orange peel, rhubarb root

NOTES
Black cherry color. Sweet with notes of smoked rhubarb and bitter orange.

TWO LUCAS, ONE LORENZO

When I was scheduling distillery tours throughout Italy to meet with amaro producers, I was disappointed that Amaro Montenegro would be closed when I was going to be in Bologna. But when I sent my itinerary to Lorenzo Tamburini, the international brand ambassador for Amaro Montenegro, to review, he had an idea. On my way to Rome, I could stop by their production plant in Teramo, the first stop for the herbs and spices used to make Montenegro. This would be Lorenzo's first visit to this facility as well, as it wasn't typically open to visitors due to the nature of the operation.

A quick sidenote: I'm terrible with directions. I did all of the driving during our distillery tours, and my traveling companion and this book's photographer, Ed Anderson, rode shotgun and manned the GPS. After each stop our hosts would ask where else we were going, and without fail, every one of them raised their eyebrows with a skeptical "why?" when we said we were going to Teramo. I was getting the feeling that Teramo was the Scranton of Italy. As we hit the road to Teramo during a summer heat wave, exhausted from jet lag and countless kilometers on the road, we were told we were just thirty minutes away from our destination. Soon, though, after many twists and turns and tight corners, our side streets narrowed down to international-thriller, Jason Bourne–style alleyways that barely fit our car. It didn't take us long to realize we had pulled into a piazza crowded with pedestrians. When the GPS instructed us to exit the vehicle and finish the journey by foot, we knew we were lost. I called the home office in Bologna to try to reach Lorenzo and, not having his surname handy, simply asked to speak with Lorenzo, which was naturally met with "Which one?" Even when we managed to get out of the piazza and to the more industrial section of town where the plant was located, it turned out the street we were trying to find had recently been renamed and didn't come up on the GPS. The plant didn't have any signs out front, but when we saw three well-dressed Italian men standing out by the gate to greet us, we knew we had arrived. Lorenzo, along with Luca Palmini, R&D and quality director, and Luca Pedretti, production plant manager, brought us inside to start our tour. I spied a folded pile of disposable lab coats and hairnets and already sweating myself silly I suited up. As a husky fellow, I felt a bit like the Hulk trying on a sport coat, and this gave Ed great amusement. After touring the factory, we went upstairs to a conference room and I was able to peel out of my lab coat. I excused myself to freshen up in the restroom, but when I got there the door was jammed. I'm sure there's a security tape on file that captured what happened next as the door became unstuck and struck me smack in the center of my forehead with a jolt. As I was washing my hands I looked in the mirror and in real time an enormous bump was forming, complete with

a trickle of blood finding its way down my sweaty forehead. Maybe all this talk about "why Teramo?" had something to it.

After some direct pressure and several bottles of water, I was able to pull myself together as we went through a tasting of infusions of all of the individual ingredients that went into making Amaro Montenegro. We were told that only three people were privy to the recipe, and I had a feeling that Luca No. 1 (Luca Palmini) was one of those people. I was on a roll with the tastings, identifying several ingredients. Luca would neither confirm nor deny my guesses, but his mischievous smile spoke volumes. I finally asked, "Luca, come on, you can tell me. You're one of the three people who know the recipe, right? Just tell me." He answered with that sly grin and the only appropriate reply in such situations, "If I told you, I'd have to kill you." And with that, we broke for lunch.

FERNET

When you hear the word *fernet*, it's likely that Fernet-Branca, the famous elixir from Milan, is what comes to mind. While Branca is undoubtedly the most popular example of this style of amaro, there are many different brands and styles of fernet on the market. Fernet-Branca wasn't even the first fernet. That honor goes to Fernet Vittone, trademarked in Milan in 1842, five years before Fernet-Branca. Still, Branca remains a household name in the category. Billy Sunday's Alex Bachman notes, "What Branca does better than anyone else is marketing. They are a powerhouse."

There is no clear designation or definition of the subcategory of fernet, but common factors include an elevated level of alcohol (typically 39 to 50 percent); a more aggressive level of bitterness; a dark brown to licorice-black color; and the use of iconic fernet herbs, spices, roots, and botanicals, including black aloe ferox, myrrh, saffron, chamomile, rhubarb root, and mint. Fernet-Branca sets the yardstick for an extremely mentholated style, but many fernets aren't as strong. But all of that being said, the lack of strict definitions, restrictions, and oversights in production in this category can be confusing. As Bachman told me, "I could walk out on the sidewalk outside the bar and do a maceration of the weeds in the cracks and call it a fernet."

The American embrace of Fernet-Branca can be traced to San Francisco, where approximately 25 percent of the Fernet-Branca imported to the United States is sold. During the past ten to fifteen years, the bartending and restaurant community adopted it as their preferred shift drink, often with a ginger beer or ginger ale back. What became known as the "bartender's handshake" traveled across the United States bar by bar, with New York City and Brooklyn catching up to San Francisco's bittersweet obsession.

British chef Fergus Henderson has been a longtime devotee of Fernet-Branca, as a restorative aid to combat hangovers and making it a steady part of his impressive day-drinking routine. One of his rituals is a daily espresso and a Fernet-Branca from his beloved Bar Italia in London's Soho district. He tells *Vanity Fair*, "It fires up the engine, improves the humors." And maybe I've got a thing for the way Brits pronounce Fernet-Branca (FAIR-net BRANK-a), but even Alfred Pennyworth, as played by Michael Caine in 2012's *The Dark Knight Rises*, is a fan of Italy's most famous fernet. In the film he entreats Bruce Wayne to hang up the Batman cloak, looking back to Batman's silent seven-year stretch. "Every year, I took a holiday. I went to Florence, there's this café on the banks of the Arno. Every fine evening I'd sit there and order a Fernet-Branca. I had this fantasy that I would look across the tables and I'd see you there, with a wife and maybe a couple of kids. You wouldn't say anything to me, nor me to you. But we'd both know that you'd made it, that you were happy."

BRANCA MENTA

Milan, Lombardy, Italy

ALCOHOL BY VOLUME
30 percent

KNOWN INGREDIENTS
Aloe ferox, chamomile, myrrh, peppermint, rhubarb root, saffron

NOTES
Dark cola color. Herbal with blasts of spearmint and peppermint.

While I was in Milan, Eduardo Branca told me the origin story of Branca Menta, a version of Fernet-Branca spiked with peppermint oil and made with more sugar and less alcohol. His grandfather, Pierluigi Branca, saw the opera singer Maria Callas in a restaurant doctoring her Fernet-Branca with mounds of crushed ice and mint leaves. She explained to Pierluigi that it was part of her preshow routine—"the ice would cool her throat, the peppermint would disinfect it, and the myrrh in Fernet-Branca expanded her pylorus," said Eduardo. Inspired by this, Fratelli Branca released Branca Menta in 1963. Branca Menta is a favorite of Eduardo's during the summer months in Italy. "Lots of ice. Delicious. We have it at every barbecue."

CONTRATTO FERNET

Canelli, Piedmont, Italy

ALCOHOL BY VOLUME
30 percent

KNOWN INGREDIENTS
Aloe ferox, anise, chamomile, cinnamon, clover, fennel, ginger, juniper berries, lemon balm, licorice, mint, myrrh, nutmeg, rhubarb root, saffron

NOTES
Dark brown color. Sweet with floral aroma and notes of licorice, saffron, and anise.

Based on a Contratto family recipe from the 1920s, this fernet contains thirty-three unique ingredients infused in a grappa base, which is then sweetened with caramelized cane sugar. It's a bit more viscous and syrupy in texture than Fernet-Branca.

FERNET-BRANCA

Milan, Lombardy, Italy

The origin of Fernet-Branca, founded by Bernardino Branca in 1845 and one of Italy's most iconic amari—sold in more than 160 countries—depends on who's telling the tale. On my visit to the historic distillery in Via Resegone in Milan, where the plant of the family-owned company has been located since 1904, Count Eduardo Branca told me, "There are two legends and it depends on who you speak to within the company. If you ask the back office, they'll tell you about two men—Mr. Fernet, a Swedish chemist, and Mr. Branca, my great-great-grandfather, an herbalist—and together they created and sold Fernet-Branca as a medicine." But if you ask the workers in the plant, you get a completely different story: "When we make fernet, you have hot and cold infusions and some of those spices, like aloe, would be mixed in hot water in an iron pail. And when you take out the iron ladle used to stir it, it would be very pale due to the chemical reaction. In Milanese dialect, *fer net* translates to 'clean iron.'"

Only the chairman of the company has complete access to the proprietary recipe of twenty-seven herbs, spices, roots, barks, and botanicals sourced from four different continents used to make up the signature formula. These ingredients—including the coal-black aloe ferox, saffron (Fratelli Branca claims to import 17 percent of the world's saffron supply, mostly from Iran), bitter orange peel, cardamom, and chamomile—are actually on full display at the Branca Museum Collection in an enormous, segmented Trivial Pursuit game piece–like installation constructed from the same Slovenian oak used for the five hundred 10-foot-tall barrels (all made by the same man until he passed away at seventy) where Fernet-Branca ages for twelve to sixteen months. Savvy visitors might notice that there are more botanicals on display than the twenty-seven that make up Fernet-Branca. Count Branca said that key ingredients from other Branca properties, including spices used to make Carpano Antica Formula, Punt e Mes, Stravecchio Branca, Sambuca, and Caffè Borghetti, were also on display. But even if you knew each and every ingredient, he noted, it wouldn't matter. "I can tell you all of them. But it's not about the spices and the herbs inside the bottle, it's all about the quantities."

Originally used as an anti-choleric—the properties of the herbs would help spark an appetite in dehydrated patients—it was "prescribed" at hospitals in Milan and sold in pharmacies in Italy up through the 1930s. The United States was the last country to sell Fernet-Branca specifically for medicinal purposes. During Prohibition, Fernet-Branca was available for sale in the United States for its purported medicinal value, a marketing point that was only used in America to help skirt the nation's strict laws. They even

ALCOHOL BY VOLUME
40 percent

KNOWN INGREDIENTS
Aloe ferox, bitter orange, cardamom, chamomile, cinchona bark, galangal, laraha, laurel, myrrh, rhubarb root, saffron, zedoaria

NOTES
Burnt caramel color. Strong and medicinal with top notes of eucalyptus. Elements of candy cane, mint toothpaste, and mentholated cough drop.

had a distribution factory in New York at 131 Hudson Street, to produce a medicinal version of Fernet-Branca, unique to the United States, from 1934 through the late 1970s. According to the 2015 book *Branca: A Spirited Italian Icon*, the Fernet-Branca sold over the counter at pharmacies in the United States was described as being "slightly different from the European version: it was slightly less alcoholic, aged for less time, and it had twice the quantity of aloe, which rendered it more bitter and enhanced both its laxative properties and its credibility as a medical remedy."

Now the only distillery outside of Italy is located in Argentina, where Fernet-Branca has achieved a cultlike status, particularly when partnered with Coca-Cola, making Fernet con cola Argentina's national cocktail. Argentina's current market share is 80 percent compared with 15 percent in Italy. Fernet-Branca was first introduced to Argentina in the 1870s to keep "Italy's gift to the world" flowing for the waves of Italian immigrants moving there. By 1925, the botanicals used to make Fernet-Branca were imported as herbal extracts from Milan to make the blend in Argentina. The current plant is now located in Tortuguitas outside of Buenos Aires.

Since its inception, Fratelli Branca has been family owned and operated, with Bernardino going into business with his three sons, Giuseppe, Luigi, and Stefano, who went on to marry Maria Scala. Throughout the generations, the company has maximized the value of advertising and marketing, collaborating with Italian and French artists to create iconic posters and advertisements. After World War II, the company created television commercials and increased outreach through collectible, branded promotional items like calendars, glassware, and ashtrays. Seventy percent of the Fernet-Branca made in Italy is exported outside the country, as the spirit of Fernet continues to spread around the world.

FERNET LAZZARONI

Saronno, Lombardy, Italy

ALCOHOL BY VOLUME
40 percent

NOTES
Dark brown color. Minty aroma with strong notes of menthol and coffee.

Founded in 1851, the historic company created Italy's famed Amaretti di Saronno cookies in addition to Lazzaroni Amaretto liqueur and Amaro Lazzaroni (see page 38). The Alpine-rich Fernet Lazzaroni became available in the United States in the summer of 2013.

FERNET VITTONE

Milan, Lombardy, Italy

Trademarked in 1842, Domenico Vittone's fernet, made up of forty proprietary herbs and spices, predates Fernet-Branca by three years, making it the first true fernet, but Fernet-Branca's commercialization and global dominance have eclipsed their claim as the "original fernet." It is newly available in the United States as of 2014. The company also produces Menta Fernet Vittone, a fernet variation flavored with peppermint (40 percent alcohol).

ALCOHOL BY VOLUME
40 percent

KNOWN INGREDIENTS
Aloe ferox, cardamom, chamomile, myrrh, rhubarb root, saffron

NOTES
Black licorice color. Classic fernet profile of peppermint, eucalyptus, and cardamom with notes of black pepper.

LUXARDO FERNET AMARO

Padua, Veneto, Italy

This fernet is a blend of fifteen herbs, spices, and botanicals made by the Luxardo family since 1889.

ALCOHOL BY VOLUME
40 percent

KNOWN INGREDIENTS
Cardamom, gentian, licorice, saffron

NOTES
Cola color. Solid balance of bitter and sweet with aromatic notes of peppermint and warm spices.

R. JELÍNEK FERNET

Luhačovice, Moravia, Czech Republic

R. Jelínek Fernet, from the producers of notable slivovitzes (plum brandies) since 1891, was created in the late nineteenth century but is fairly new to the United States. It is much milder than the bracing Fernet-Branca.

ALCOHOL BY VOLUME
38 percent

NOTES
Dark amber color. Notes of cinnamon, baking spices, anise.

TEMPUS FUGIT SPIRITS FERNET DEL FRATE ANGELICO

Kallnach, Bern, Switzerland

ALCOHOL BY VOLUME
44 percent

KNOWN INGREDIENTS
Aloe ferox, angelica, gentian, mint, myrrh, saffron

NOTES
Tea-colored. Dry with floral notes and strong herbal bitterness.

Founded by John Troia and Peter Schaf, Tempus Fugit Spirits, in California, has been in the business of bringing back long-lost historical spirits. Their fernet expression, released in 2013, based on a historical recipe purchased by a Swiss distiller from the Cusatelli Distillery in Milan in 1930, is produced in small batches at the Matter Luginbühl Distillery in Kallnach, Switzerland. Troia notes that based on correspondence from the 1930s, the original fernet, which had been made since the early 1880s, was "the first indication of a monk with the last name of Fernét being associated with fernet" and points out that among the so-called counterfeit bottles of fernet that line an entire wall at the Fernet-Branca museum, there is a bottle with a monk on the label. Troia adds, "This isn't our interpretation of fernet; it's preserved and presented as a historic relic from the 1880s." Alex Bachman of Chicago's Billy Sunday is a fan: "Fernet Angelico is the best modern iteration of fernet available in the U.S. market."

SALMIAKKI DALA SCANDINAVIAN FERNET

Mosfellsbær, Iceland

ALCOHOL BY VOLUME
38 percent

KNOWN INGREDIENTS
Aloe ferox, anise, chicory, licorice root, saffron, sal ammoniac

NOTES
Black coffee color. Astringent with savory notes and a salty finish.

Launched in 2014 by DALA Spirits—a subsidiary of Bittermens Inc. and Bittermens Spirits—this Scandinavian fernet gets its name from sal ammoniac, the natural version of ammonium chloride, the primary ingredient in the salty licorice popular in Nordic countries.

FERNET-VALLET

Santiago Tulantepec, Hidalgo, Mexico

ALCOHOL BY VOLUME
35 percent

KNOWN INGREDIENTS
Cardamom, cinnamon, clove, gentian, mint, orange peel, quassia, rhubarb root

NOTES
Black cherry in color. Very bitter. Herbal Alpine spices with burst of menthol and notes of warm molasses.

After the short-lived reign of Maximilian I of Mexico, the French monarch who was executed by firing squad in 1867, many French émigrés, including Henri Vallet, chose to stay in their adopted homeland. By the 1880s, Vallet had used his chemistry background to gain renown as a distiller and creator of bitter liqueurs, of which his Fernet-Vallet and Amargo-Vallet are still being produced.

CH FERNET-DOGMA

Chicago, Illinois, United States

After creating their take on an American amaro (see page 80) in 2015, CH Distillery partnered with Chicago bartenders Clint Rogers, Alex Renshaw, and Brian Sturgulewski of the Dogma Group, a local hospitality and beverage consulting boutique, to launch a Midwest fernet that's aged in Four Roses bourbon barrels. Taking a cue from the Italian custom of partnering fernet and espresso, Tremaine Atkinson, CH Distillery's cofounder and master distiller, sourced coffee beans from local Dark Matter Coffee as well as chamomile and other botanicals from the Rare Tea Cellar in the nearby Ravenswood neighborhood of Chicago. "It's a take on classic Italian fernet in its combination of bitter, herbal, and minty flavors," says Atkinson. "What sets it apart is the clarity of these flavors—they are not buried in sweetness like many fernets."

ALCOHOL BY VOLUME
38.4 percent

KNOWN INGREDIENTS
Chamomile, coffee, eucalyptus, lemon peel, rose flower, saffron

NOTES
Espresso color. Coffee. Herbaceous, minty, light bitterness. Barrel-aged. Minty, lightly bitter.

FALCON SPIRITS FERNET FRANCISCO

Richmond, California, United States

After first meeting at the Southern California music festival Coachella, longtime amaro enthusiast Max Rudsten and winemaker Ben Flajnik collaborated with Falcon Spirits' master distiller Farid Dormishian to create the Bay Area's first locally made fernet. Two years later, their bittersweet "local, approachable fernet" came to market, made from twelve locally sourced ingredients, through a process of blending a non-GMO natural-grain corn spirit with herbal infusions of grape-based brandy. "We wanted to highlight local ingredients and give a region that loves fernet their own expression of terroir," offers Flajnik. Rudsten adds, "As a local guy, I wanted to create a fernet the city could call its own. After all, we do consume more of it than any city in the United States. Ask anyone and they always remember their first taste of fernet. There's emotion attached to it. It takes hold of your senses and gives you an incredible jolt. It sparks a curiosity that very few spirits can match."

ALCOHOL BY VOLUME
40 percent

KNOWN INGREDIENTS
Angelica root, bay leaf, cardamom, chamomile, cinnamon, gentian, orange peel, orris root, peppermint, rhubarb root, spearmint

NOTES
Espresso color. Dry and woody with a strong mint profile.

FERNET LEOPOLD HIGHLAND AMARO

Denver, Colorado, United States

ALCOHOL BY VOLUME
40 percent

KNOWN INGREDIENTS
Aloe ferox, bergamot, black pepper, blackstrap molasses, chamomile, cocoa nibs, dandelion root, elderflower, gentian root, ginger, honeysuckle, lavender, peppermint, rose petals, sarsaparilla, vanilla

NOTES
Black licorice color. Strong and bitter with dominant mint profile with notes of chocolate and coffee.

Inspired by a conversation with Atlanta barman Greg Best, Colorado distiller Todd Leopold put a decidedly Rocky Mountain spin on the classic fernet profile and created the first American-made fernet since Prohibition. Launched in December 2011, the small-batch blend of more than twenty botanicals includes three different types of mint along with cocoa nibs and sarsaparilla and is aged for six months in chardonnay barrels from Napa Valley. It has a unique and sometimes polarizing profile; it's miles away from being just another Fernet-Branca clone. Odell Brewing in Fort Collins, Colorado, has been filling those empty fernet barrels with their imperial porter for its Fernet Aged Porter—a limited release available each January.

LETHERBEE FERNET

Chicago, Illinois, United States

ALCOHOL BY VOLUME
35 percent

KNOWN INGREDIENTS
Aloe ferox, cardamom, eucalyptus, fennel, gentian, licorice root, mugwort, myrrh gum, peppermint, rhubarb root, saffron, spearmint, wormwood

NOTES
Deep, dark brown. Bitter, mentholated, and slightly medicinal but smooth with oily texture.

Before founding Chicago's Letherbee Distillers, Brenton Engel was making moonshine at his Springfield, Illinois, farmhouse and sharing his hooch among Chicago's top bartenders, where it developed a cult following. Now, with distiller Nathan Ozug and Ian Van Veen, Letherbee makes limited-edition seasonal bottlings of gin in addition to their bitter take on Chicago's love-it-or-hate-it wormwood liqueur, Malört (see page 83). In the summer of 2014, they launched their local take on the industry favorite with a blend of more than twenty herbs and botanicals lightly sweetened with caramelized beet sugar.

SKIN-DEEP

"That first sip I took of Fernet was long before I was a bartender and I was like, 'What the fuck is this?' Then thirty minutes later I was like, 'Where'd that bottle go? Let's do that again.'"

Damon Boelte wears his love of Fernet-Branca like a badge of honor. Literally. Emblazoned across his chest is a tableau of a fierce and determined eagle with a bottle of booze in its talons, inspired by the iconic symbol of Fernet-Branca created by Leopoldo Metlicovitz in 1893. "I'm really into Americana and classic- and traditional-style tattoo work. A lot of guys around the World War II era would have a tattoo of an eagle on their chests for a symbol of pride or allegiance. I remember looking at the Fernet label and the Fernet eagle was carrying the bottle around the planet. Companies in the eighteenth and nineteenth centuries often had eagles as their logos—a very strong, powerful image. What I like about the Fernet-Branca logo is that it's essentially medicine. The idea of an eagle carrying medicine around the world struck me as something I could get behind. I didn't want my Fernet-Branca tattoo to be the actual image. I wanted to put my own spin on it. The content is the same, but the style is different. People never notice this but on the back of the Fernet bottle it says, 'Excellence knows no oceans, no frontiers.' I can dig that."

DOWN WITH THE COUNT

When I arranged a private tour of the Fratelli Branca Distillerie in Milan, the public relations contact in New York gave me the address and said to check in with the guard at the gate and ask for Eduardo. The Fernet-Branca offices and factory take up an entire city block, and when I stepped out of my taxi, I marked my own version of the stations of the cross, pausing in the street to look up at the ornate iron plaque of their logo—with that iconic, bottle-clutching eagle flying around the globe—looming over the building's garage and loading dock. The blast of a horn from a delivery truck pulling out of the garage broke my reverie, and I went inside, handed over my passport to the security guard, and asked for Eduardo. I was directed to wait in the next room with saffron-colored walls, and after a few minutes, Eduardo descended from his second-floor office and ambled down the long staircase, underplaying a backdrop made for grand entrances.

He was in his early thirties and dressed in khakis and a blue-and-white pin-striped button-down with a tie. His hair was a little rumpled and a small bandage covered a shaving nick on his neck. We said hello and quickly launched into the tour. At first I thought he was brought up from the marketing bullpen or someone from the front desk asked to give yet another tour to a visiting Fernet-Branca enthusiast. He warmed up talking about the twenty-seven herbs and spices and botanicals used to make their formula, "Aloe brings the bitterness, but he's a naughty boy. He takes a lot longer to amalgamate with the other spices." As he was describing the archival glassware and collectibles on display in a locked cabinet, a dashing man I recognized as Count Niccolò Branca di Romanico, the fifth-generation scion of the family dynasty, swept into the room. He was in jeans, a crisp white shirt with an extra button undone, wearing dark-rimmed glasses, a royal blue sport coat with complementary pocket square, and in possession of an enviable mane of windblown salt-and-pepper hair. A gaggle of small Italian children followed in his wake, adding to the "just walked off a Fellini movie set" vibe that took over the room. The elder Count nodded my way, then took a set of keys from his pocket, opened the case, and palmed a glass from the museum display case, tucked it in his pocket, and went on his way. "My father, he does that sometimes," Eduardo explained, and then it hit me like a shot of Fernet, this guy whom I had pegged as the Milanese version of Jim Halpert from *The Office* was in fact Count Eduardo Branca.

After the tour of the museum and the aromatic cellar lined with oak barrels, and a brief peek at the working production line, we stopped in their barroom and had a Fernet. Eduardo said that he had been traveling around the world promoting Fernet-Branca and had seen it consumed in so many different ways. "In Italy, France, Germany, and Spain, it's a digestif, sipped after a meal. The Northern countries like it as a morning drink—a breakfast shot of Fernet. But English-speaking countries—the U.S., U.K., and Australia—you're a shot and cocktail culture." It didn't seem to be a judgment call, but instead an acknowledgment, and perhaps appreciation, of the versatility of his family's storied elixir.

A BITTERSWEET WORLD

While the word *amaro* is distinctly Italian, the tradition of consuming an herbal, bittersweet liqueur as an aperitif or digestif extends to other countries, particularly in France (*amer*), Germany (*Kräuterlikör*), Spain (*amargo*), and other European countries like the Netherlands, Hungary, and the Czech Republic. There are countless variations of brands sold around the world, and while the selection in the United States keeps improving, there are too many to name that still aren't yet available here. Some of those include Amer Picon (France), Gammel Dansk (Denmark), Appenzeller (Switzerland), Riga Black Balsam (Latvia), Pelinkovac (Croatia), and Wurzelpeter (Germany). But here's a look at some of the brands and styles from abroad that are available. Turn to page 77 for a look ahead to America's homegrown amaro movement.

JÄGERMEISTER

Wolfenbüttel, Lower Saxony, Germany

ALCOHOL BY VOLUME
35 percent

KNOWN INGREDIENTS
bitter orange peel, cardamom, cinnamon, ginger, licorice root, star anise

NOTES
Dark golden brown color. An herbal blast of mentholated bitterness with notes of licorice, anise, and spicy cinnamon.

The iconic green bottle emblazoned with a cross glowing over the head of a giant white stag was likely many Americans' first foray into the world of bittersweet liqueurs. One of the top ten best-selling spirits worldwide, Jägermeister was created in 1934 by Curt Mast, an avid hunter (the cross and stag are references to Saint Hubertus and Saint Eustace, respectively, patron saints of hunters), who, after his father's death, added the production of spirits to his family's vinegar factory.

Made from a secret blend of fifty-six herbs, fruit, spices, flowers, barks, and botanicals and aged for a year in oak barrels made from wood harvested from the Palatinate Forest, Jägermeister was only available in Germany until the 1960s, when it began to be exported throughout Europe. In 1974, American Sidney Frank, who died in 2006, began importing Jägermeister to America through his namesake Sidney Frank Importing Company. He played a pivotal role in giving the staid German digestif a makeover, making it the go-to shot, served ice cold, for revelers of all ages. In recent years, the brand has been moving away from their party image. The sexy Jägerettes and hunky Jäger Dudes, who served as the front line in brand adoption and promotional efforts, have been retired in a bid for respectability as a versatile ingredient behind the bar.

KUEMMERLING

Bodenheim, Rhineland-Palatinate, Germany

In 1921, Hugo Kümmerling invented a mild herbal bitter, and by 1938, he perfected the recipe that has been in production in Deesbach, Germany, since 1963. The family-owned company sells Kuemmerling in 20-milliliter single-serve bottles in multipacks, as well as a 500-millliter bottle.

ALCOHOL BY VOLUME
35 percent

KNOWN INGREDIENTS
Allspice, angelica root, calamus, cinnamon bark, clove, guaiac resin, licorice root, spearmint, wormwood

NOTES
Dark brown color. Dominant flavor of licorice and cloves.

SCHWARTZHOG KRÄUTER LIQUEUR

Nörten-Hardenberg, Lower Saxony, Germany

The Hardenberg-Wilthen distillery in Nörten-Hardenberg, Germany, home to Schwartzhog Kräuter Liqueur, has been owned by the same family since the 1700s. Based on a medieval recipe, the herbal liqueur's name translates to "black hog," which is emblazoned on the Hardenberg family crest. With an eye on the Jägermeister market, to "shoot the hog" is an invitation to knock back an ice-cold shot. Mix it with Red Bull and you've got yourself a Hog Bomb.

ALCOHOL BY VOLUME
36.7 percent

KNOWN INGREDIENTS
Gentian, ginger, wormwood

NOTES
Cola color. Strong notes of ginger, cinnamon, and citrus.

UNDERBERG

Rheinberg, Wesel, Germany

In June 17, 1846, on the same day that he married Catharina Albrecht, Hubert Underberg founded Underberg-Albrecht in Rheinberg, Germany, to produce his namesake herbal digestif, which is made from ingredients sourced from forty-three different countries and aged in casks made of Slovenian oak. His elixir was available in various bottle sizes until 1949, when, to combat counterfeits and create an on-the-go digestif, his grandson Emil Underberg oversaw the design of the single-serve bottle. This now iconic 20-milliliter bottle, wrapped in khaki-colored paper and topped with a green twist cap, is sold on its own, in three-packs, in collectible tins, or by the case. The loyalty program for Underberg drinkers around the world invites enthusiasts to collect and send in their green bottle caps in exchange for a host of Underberg-branded curiosities, including drinking glasses, playing cards, metal signs, a toy truck with trailer to cart your miniature bottles, and a slick leather bandolier loaded with Underberg "bullets."

ALCOHOL BY VOLUME
44 percent

KNOWN INGREDIENTS
Gentian

NOTES
Dark amber color. A wash of alpine-flecked christmas spices with heavy notes of clove, chamomile, and licorice.

UNDERBERG: ANY WAY YOU WANT IT, THAT'S THE WAY YOU NEED IT

I have a bit of an obsession with Underberg, and for a number of years now, I've done my best to behave like a bittersweet Johnny Appleseed, stuffing my jacket pockets with the single-serve bottles to serve as the ultimate icebreaker and leaving a trail of green bottle caps and torn paper wrappers in my wake. My position as honorary Underberg missionary began when I was first introduced to Underberg and the rituals surrounding its enjoyment at my local, Prime Meats, in Brooklyn. Traditionally, Underberg is served at the end of a meal alongside a tall glass. The contents of the bottle are poured into the glass and knocked back in one shot—no sipping. You can also twist the paper wrapper to make a custom handle and take it straight from the bottle, though the little hiccup of air fighting to get through the tiny opening can interrupt the flow. At Prime Meats, most customers receive the tall glass treatment, but for regulars, their Underberg is delivered with a little black bar straw poking out of the bottle. Taking it down in one suck, so to speak, increases the intensity of that warm Alpine rush and eliminates the need to wash an extra glass. Damon Boelte popularized this service method during his tenure at the bar. "The straw in the bottle is definitely my thing. That's 'Prime Meats style.' We ushered that into the cocktail world. People look to it as part of our program."

Boelte was one of the first to popularize Underberg as a cocktail ingredient (see the Alpine Sour, page 114) and Prime Meats is also where I first saw an Underberg bottle employed as a garnish, adorning a boozy slushy from Garret Richard called the Ice-Berg (page 165), which made its debut on the menu of a tiki takeover at the bar.

But it's not just a Brooklyn thing. The staff at Edmund's Oast in Charleston, South Carolina, have taken their Underberg appreciation to the next level. Head bartender Jayce McConnell ordered one hundred cases of Underberg (three thousand bottles) and deposited the contents of each bottle into a barrel that previously held Charleston's High Wire Distilling's sorghum whiskey as well as a house-made "strong, dark wheat ale called Nameless City." After six months of resting, the barrel-aged Underberg was rebottled in single-serve bottles, an imperial stout called Pub Lurker was added to the barrel, and after three months' rest was rechristened as Underlurker. And David Little, of Seattle's Barnacle, turned me on to the UnderServe from the Denver pizzeria Cart-Driver, in which an order of soft-serve ice cream is presented in a glass with an Underberg garnish.

I have Boelte to thank for turning me on to Underberg, but he's quick to counter, "Underberg has been around since 1846. I can't take much credit for its popularity."

AVÈZE

Riom-ès-Montagnes, Cantal, France

ALCOHOL BY VOLUME
20 percent

KNOWN INGREDIENTS
Gentian

NOTES
Floral and grassy with notes of anise, pine, and orange peel.

This French aperitif was created in 1929 by Émile Refouvelet, sourcing wild gentian roots from the Auvergne Volcanoes Regional Park in Aydat, whose volcanic mountains are featured on the bottle's label.

BÄSKA SNAPS MED MALÖRT

La Cluse-et-Mijoux, Franche-Comté, France

ALCOHOL BY VOLUME
40 percent

KNOWN INGREDIENTS
Caraway, citrus, licorice root, wormwood

NOTES
Copper color. Sharp and bitter and with sweet, herbal notes.

This Swedish-style bitter spirit from DALA Spirits was formulated by Bittermens cofounder Avery Glasser and produced and bottled in France's famed Distillerie Les Fils d'Emile Pernot by blending a custom aquavit with a wormwood distillate. It's best enjoyed chilled or straight from the freezer, or in a cocktail like the Boss Colada (page 129).

BIGALLET CHINA-CHINA AMER LIQUEUR

Panissage, Isère, France

ALCOHOL BY VOLUME
40 percent

KNOWN INGREDIENTS
Anise, bitter orange peel, cinchona bark, clove, gentian, sweet orange peel

NOTES
Molasses color. Spicy with notes of burnt orange and mint.

In 1872, Felix Bigallet founded his distillery in Lyon, where he made syrups and liqueurs for nearby restaurants and cafés. The recipe for Bigallet China-China Amer Liqueur dates back to 1875, and the mix of bitter and sweet orange peels are distilled three times in copper alembic stills, resulting in a deep orange flavor as well as a higher alcohol count.

SALERS APERITIF LA BOUNOUX GENTIANE LIQUEUR

Salers, Cantal, France

ALCOHOL BY VOLUME
16 percent

KNOWN INGREDIENTS
Gentian

NOTES
Light gold color. Vegetal, grassy, citrus, anise, and forest floor.

This is one of the oldest aperitifs from the Massif Central region of France. It was invented by Ambroise Labounoux in 1885 and uses yellow gentian root from the slopes of the Auvergne volcanoes.

SUZE SAVEUR D'AUTREFOIS

Thuir, Pyrénées-Orientales, France

Invented in 1885 by Parisian distiller Fernand Moreaux and first sold commercially in 1889, Suze, the oldest gentian-based liqueur from the Massif Central region, is made up of 50 percent gentian root harvested by hand from the Auvergne. Pernod Ricard has owned the brand since 1965, and it became available in the United States in 2012.

ALCOHOL BY VOLUME
20 percent

KNOWN INGREDIENTS
Gentian root

NOTES
Light amber color. Earthy with spicy notes of orange peel. Floral, lemon notes.

WOLFBERGER WOLFAMER LIQUEUR A L'ORANGE

Colmar, Alsace, France

This aromatic, bittersweet orange liqueur, from the historic Wolfberger distillery in the French Alsace region bordering Germany and Switzerland, is versatile on its own, in a cocktail, served over the rocks with soda, or added to a lager for a classic *amer bière*. Other *amer* variations from Wolfberger include the ginger-spiked Wolfberger Amer Ginembre (18 percent alcohol by volume), and Wolfberger Amer Fleur de Joie (18 percent alcohol by volume), made with hops, gentian root, cinchona bark, citrus, cinnamon, clove, and *amer eau de vie de bière* (beer brandy).

ALCOHOL BY VOLUME
21 percent

KNOWN INGREDIENTS
Cinchona bark, gentian root, orange peel

NOTES
Amber color. Mild bitterness. Slightly syrupy with notes of citrus and spice.

BECHEROVKA

Karlovy Vary, Bohemia, Czech Republic

Karlovy Vary, the West Bohemia spa town home to thirteen hot springs, whose mineral waters are renowned for their professed curative powers, is also where the herbal liqueur Becherovka was born. It was launched in 1807 as Becher's English Bitter, based on a formula developed by pharmacist Josef Vitus Becher and British-born doctor Christian Frobrig, and popularized in 1838 when Becher's son, Johann Becher, helped transition the bitter from being taken as a medicine to being enjoyed as a liqueur. After World War II, the company was taken over and run by the state, with privatization returning in 2001. In 2011, the company was purchased by Pernod Ricard and soon gained wider distribution in the United States. The proprietary recipe is known to only two people in the company, who meet every Wednesday in isolation to oversee the blending of the more than twenty botanicals. After macerating, it matures in oak barrels for four weeks. Typically served chilled on its own or with a beer chaser, or when mixed with tonic and lemon as a *beton*, translated as "concrete."

ALCOHOL BY VOLUME
38 percent

NOTES
Pale yellow pilsner color. Mentholated medicinal with notes of bark, clove, ginger, cinnamon, honey, and orange peel.

R. JELÍNEK AMARO LIQUEUR

Luhačovice, Moravia, Czech Republic

ALCOHOL BY VOLUME
30 percent

NOTES
*Dark copper color.
Floral and citrusy with
mild level of bitterness.*

Newly available in the United States to partner with their fernet (see page 55), this amaro from R. Jelínek is on the lighter side of the bitter scale.

ZWACK UNICUM LIQUEUR

Budapest, Hungary

ALCOHOL BY VOLUME
40 percent

NOTES
*Dark tawny brown
color. Strong,
herbaceous bitterness
with notes of cinnamon
and orange peel.*

Unicum, the national shot of Hungary, was created in 1790 by Dr. József Zwack, the royal physician to the Imperial Court of Holy Roman Emperor Joseph II. In 1840, J. Zwack and Co. was founded, making their blend of more than twenty secret herbs and botanicals, aged for six months in oak barrels, the country's first commercial liquor company. From 1899 to 1922, through an agreement with the Red Cross, the Zwack family paid for permission through donations to use the iconic red cross on the labels of their distinctive round bottles, but after the agreement ended they switched to a gold cross. Their factory was bombed three different times during World War II, halting production, and when the Communist Party took over, it nationalized the business in 1948. The fifth-generation brothers, Béla and János Zwack, took divergent paths. János left the country for America with the original family recipe smuggled in his jacket pocket, while Béla was put to work at the family factory, supplying a less-than-accurate version of the actual formula to use for production. In 1988, János's son, Péter Zwack, returned with his family to Hungary, and in 1991, he bought back the family business, which is now run by his children, Sandor and Izabella Zwack.

Where it gets a little confusing is that in Hungary the product based on the original 1790 formula is known as Unicum. The product for export is branded with the family name, Zwack. After years of limited distribution in the United States, Diageo purchased the brand, and the current version of Unicum sold is called Zwack Liqueur (or Unicum Next for European markets). This 40 percent alcohol-by-volume version, launched in 2004, was modified to appeal to the U.S. market by making it lighter in color and sweeter than the bitter original, with a pronounced citrus-forward profile. Also available since 2012 is Zwack Unicum Plum Liqueur (35 percent alcohol), which is Zwack liqueur aged for six months in oak casks filled with dried plums, resulting in a portlike product.

AMARO DI ANGOSTURA

Laventille, Trinidad and Tobago, West Indies

ALCOHOL BY VOLUME
35 percent

NOTES
*Burnt caramel color.
Christmas spice
profile of cinnamon,
clove, nutmeg, and
cardamom with herbal,
root beer sweetness.*

As the trend of bartenders knocking back full-ounce shots of Angostura bitters continues to spread, it makes sense that Angostura elected to get into the potable amaro game. The first amaro from the House of Angostura was unveiled in July 2014 during Tales of the Cocktail, the annual drinks industry event, then rolled out nationally in early 2015. Long known for their iconic yellow-capped cocktail bitters invented in 1824, as well as for being producers of rum, Amaro di Angostura was created by an all-female team and is said to be inspired by Carlos Siegert, the son of Angostura founder J. G. B. Siegert. Like the bitters, the recipe is kept a secret, but the House of Angostura does share that Angostura aromatic bitters are blended with a neutral spirit to create the base of the amaro.

AMARGO-VALLET BARK OF ANGOSTURA APERITIVO LIQUEUR

Santiago Tulantepec, Hidalgo, Mexico

ALCOHOL BY VOLUME
45 percent

KNOWN INGREDIENTS
*Angostura bark,
cherries, cloves*

NOTES
*Black plum color.
Flavor of medicinal
roots and bark
with notes of dark,
bittersweet chocolate,
dried cherry, and
coffee.*

Despite its name, there is no angostura bark in Angostura bitters. But that's not the case with Amargo-Vallet, as angostura bark is the primary ingredient in this high-proof companion amaro to Henri Vallet's Fernet-Vallet (see page 56). Rounded out with a maceration of dried cherries and spices, it's the potable Angostura bitters you always wanted, but with a much more versatile profile, making it ideal on its own or used in place of vermouth in a Manhattan.

AROMATIZED AND FORTIFIED WINES

While there are some wine-based vino amaro such as Cardamaro and Cappelletti Elisir Novasalus, the category of low-alcohol aromatized and fortified aperitif wines can be considered kissing cousins to amaro. Aromatized wines are infused with herbs and botanicals for additional flavor and color, while a fortified wine is spiked with a neutral spirit like unaged brandy to raise the alcohol percentage of the wine. Once opened, these wines will begin to oxidize, and while they will lose their intensity and complexity, they can keep in the refrigerator for up to a month.

VERMOUTH An essential ingredient in cocktails like the martini, Manhattan, and Negroni, vermouth was born in the Alpine areas of Italy's Piedmont region and France's Savoy region. The word is derived from the German word for wormwood (*wermut*), which is the traditional bittering agent for European vermouth and was consumed as a tonic to treat intestinal worms. Additional herbs and botanicals used in vermouth making include chamomile, cinnamon, marjoram, and citrus peels. Sugar is also added to vermouth and the alcohol-by-volume range is 14.5 to 22 percent. New-look American vermouths aren't regulated by European Union rules, so they can be more flexible with their use of wormwood and still call themselves a vermouth. For further reading on the topic, turn to Atsby Vermouth founder Adam Ford's *Vermouth: The Revival of the Spirit That Created America's Cocktail Culture* or *The Mixellany Guide to Vermouth and Other Aperitifs* by Jared Brown and Anistatia Miller.

QUINQUINA This category derives its name from *quina*, the Incan word for the Peruvian cinchona bark from which quinine is produced. Quinquinas originated as a tonic to help make bitter quinine more palatable. Examples of this style include Bonal Gentiane-Quina (France), Lillet Blanc (France), Byrrh Grand Quinquina (France), Dubonnet (France), and Kina L'Aero d'Or (Switzerland).

AMERICANO *Americano* doesn't refer to the cocktail, the coffee drink, or a nickname for a visiting American, it comes from *americante*, which means "bittered" in Italian. This category (or subcategory of quinquina) must contain gentian root. Examples of this style include Cocchi Americano Bianco (Italy), Cocchi Americano Rosa (Italy), Contratto Americano Rosso (Italy), and Cappelletti Aperitivo Americano Rosso (Italy).

BAROLO CHINATO Traditionally served as a digestif at the end of a meal (especially when paired with chocolate) rather than as an aperitif, Barolo Chinato is a fortified wine from Piedmont, Italy, that came about in the late nineteenth century using one of Italy's most noted wines—made from Nebbiolo grapes—as a base. The wine is then aromatized with cinchona bark and other botanicals like ginger, rhubarb, orange peel, and cloves. Noted producers of Barolo Chinato from Piedmont include Cocchi, Cappellano, Barale, and Marcarini.

BITTER LONDON

On a trip to London, I was having a difficult time ordering an amaro beyond Fernet-Branca at the end of dinner. I'd rattle off the usual suspects like Averna or Montenegro, and the waiter would disappear for a while and then come back empty-handed. Several bartender friends told me to seek out Gerry's Wines and Spirits, a jam-packed shop on Old Compton Street in Soho, and after quizzing the manager on amaro, he waved me behind the counter, "Have a look." I dug through the bottles on the shelves and climbed over the boxes in the cramped aisles but didn't uncover any unexpected amari. He asked if I was a bartender back in the States. I told him I was a drinks writer and gave him my card. "Brad Thomas Parsons . . . Ah, you're the geezer who wrote the bitters book? Well, let's have a drink," he said, lining up some bottles with the full intention of getting me smashed before I departed. Full disclosure: he succeeded.

Later that night at a hotel bar, I asked the white-jacketed barman about the dearth of amaro in London. He explained that traditionally they preferred sweeter drinks at the end of the meal, particularly port. But he did say things were changing a bit, and as proof, brought down a bottle of Kamm and Sons, a ginseng-based British aperitif that was starting to show up in bars and restaurants around London. Created in 2011 after five years in development by London bartender Alex Kammerling, Kamm and Sons packs more than forty botanicals, including four different kinds of ginseng, wormwood, gentian root, elderflower, grapefruit peel, echinacea, fennel seeds, hibiscus flowers, goji berries, juniper berries, and honey, combining the distillation process of a London-style gin with the tradition of Italian aperitivo bitters like Campari and Aperol.

Another sign that London is beginning to embrace bitter comes via brothers Rob and Jim Asterley, who are developing Asterley Bros. Dispense Amaro. Rob married into a Sicilian family and was given a recipe for a homegrown Italian amaro. The brothers have been beta testing their progression to create a "modern British amaro" using British hops, orange and grapefruit peels, rhubarb, lime, basil, rosemary, gentian root, wormwood, and a host of other botanicals.

Hopefully both of these brands will make the trip across the Atlantic and become available in the United States.

AMERICAN-MADE AMARO

Throughout my exploration of the world of amaro, my desire to see more American distillers craft their own regional takes on Italy's indigenous bittersweet liqueur has only increased. With the boom in craft distilling across the country, I long for examples of a great Pacific Northwest amaro flavored with pine needles and smoked alder or a Southern amaro spiked with pecans and sweetened with sorghum. Thankfully, more brands and labels are hitting liquor shelves, but the category presents many challenges that inhibit the average gin or white whiskey distiller from jumping into the bittersweet amaro game.

Nicholas Finger of Brooklyn's St. Agrestis Amaro says, "Amaro is a challenging product not only to make but to sell. You're never going to get rich off it because the market is so small, so in turn, you really have to love it to even think about making it. Everyone knows whiskey and gin and drinks them all the time. Amaro is such a specialty product that it's only going to appeal to a few people."

Tremaine Atkinson, cofounder and master distiller at Chicago's CH Distillery, agrees. "Amaro is a very different production process than traditional distilled spirits, which is what most craft distillers are focused on. Amaro is also a tougher sell to the general public because it's complex and so unlike most other spirits."

Lance Winters, of St. George Spirits in Alameda, California, has also been at work on a house amaro. "There are probably a ton of reasons for the dearth of domestically made amaro. The prime reason is that with all the layers of complexity in a good amaro it's really difficult to do well. Most of the new distillers lack the experience to execute. It's also not a high-volume spirit. Most of the new distilleries are busy trying to distill the things that will provide the cash flow they need to survive. Once that's established, we'll probably see more of them venturing into the amaro territory."

John Troia, cofounder of California's Tempus Fugit Spirits, has concerns on what really makes ingredients local or regional. "What would distinguish a domestic amaro from a European amaro other than its geography? If I'm in the Pacific Northwest, I'm still grabbing bitter orange peels, I'm still grabbing gentian root. What is it about that region that would distinguish itself? That's what would be more compelling. If I was in Georgia, maybe local Georgia peaches as a signature flavor would speak to the regional terroir."

Billy Sunday's Alex Bachman, proprietor of America's largest selection of amaro, says, "Through time we'll see more local production, but Italy and western Europe have hundreds of years of experience with production and sourcing botanicals. It's an unfamiliar category from the consumer standpoint, and we have no history or standard of manufacturing amaro. The skill set to understand maceration is a lifetime of work. It's really just beginning. American palates are getting on board, but it's a little plant that we're trying to nurse into growth."

ART IN THE AGE ROOT LIQUEUR

Tamworth, New Hampshire, United States

ALCOHOL BY VOLUME
40 percent

KNOWN INGREDIENTS
Allspice, birch bark, cardamom, clove, lemon peel, nutmeg, orange peel, smoked black tea, spearmint, star anise, wintergreen

NOTES
Root beer color. Aromatic sweetness with notes of vanilla, birch bark, and a peppery herbal kick.

Inspired by Native American root-tea elixirs made of birch bark, herbs, and sarsaparilla that were once spirituous but later evolved into what we now know as root beer, Steven Grasse, founder of the Philadelphia-based Art in the Age, created Root, an organic bittersweet liqueur that's produced at Tamworth Distilling in Tamworth, New Hampshire.

BALSAM AMERICAN AMARO

Glenshaw, Pennsylvania, United States

ALCOHOL BY VOLUME
44 percent

KNOWN INGREDIENTS
Cinnamon, clove, tea leaves, wormwood

NOTES
Dark brown color. Earthy, bitter, aromatic, anise, chocolate, baking spices.

Balsam American Amaro is the tag-team effort of Rodrick Markus, owner of Chicago's Rare Tea Cellar, Chicago bartender and Hum Spirits founder Adam Seger, and Barry Young, the master distiller at Pennsylvania Pure Distilleries. The concentrated amaro is made from more than thirty ingredients macerated in a base of Boyd and Blair 151-proof potato vodka. Beyond sipping it neat, this concentrated amaro also serves as a base ingredient to turn wine into vermouth, either by the bottle or the glass. Their efforts were worth the wait, as their first run of three thousand bottles released in the spring of 2015 sold out within two hours. Award-winning chefs like Grant Achatz, Paul Kahan, Eric Ripert, and Daniel Humm were among those who scooped up the new amaro.

BITTERMENS SPIRITS AMÈRE NOUVELLE

Westfield, New York, United States

ALCOHOL BY VOLUME
30 percent

KNOWN INGREDIENTS
Bitter orange, gentian

NOTES
Golden color. Bitter orange with a hint of sweetness rounded out with aromatic spices.

In 2011, Bittermens founders Avery and Janet Glasser, the makers of notable cocktail bitters in flavors like Hopped Grapefruit and Xocolatl Mole, partnered with Mayur Subbarao, a vermouth and cordial formulator, to launch Bittermens Spirits. Looking to fill the gap in availability of the category of *amer fleur de bière* liqueurs, which includes Amer Picon, in the United States, this Alsatian-inspired liqueur is higher in proof, much like the original Amer Picon without the burnt caramel sweetness.

BITTERMENS SPIRITS AMÈRE SAUVAGE

Westfield, New York, United States

Inspired by the key bittering agent in most amaro and bitters, Amère Sauvage is made using French yellow gentian root in a style that harks back to the original version of the gentian-based aperitif Suze (see page 69).

ALCOHOL BY VOLUME
23 percent

KNOWN INGREDIENTS
Gentian root

NOTES
Copper color. Woodsy and bitter, rounded out with floral citrus.

BITTERMENS SPIRITS CITRON SAUVAGE

Westfield, New York, United States

Bittermens describes its bitter grapefruit liqueur as tasting "like summer in a glass." Use it in cocktails as you would a triple sec or top off with soda for an aperitif.

ALCOHOL BY VOLUME
16 percent

KNOWN INGREDIENTS
Gentian, grapefruit

NOTES
Dark copper color. Floral with mild citrus-driven bitterness.

BRECKENRIDGE BITTERS

Breckenridge, Colorado, United States

Breckenridge Bitters, created in 2012 by Bryan Nolt and master distiller Jordan Via, hails from its namesake Colorado ski resort town, making it home to the highest distillery in the world at 9,600 feet above sea level. Sixteen herbs, fruits, and botanicals, many picked from Colorado's Tenmile Range, reflect an American interpretation of a classic Alpine-style amaro. Sip it neat or mix it into a cocktail, or try their pro tip and drop a shot of their bitters into a glass of IPA with a shot for a Rocky Mountain spin on a classic *amer bière.*

ALCOHOL BY VOLUME
36 percent

KNOWN INGREDIENTS
Génépi, gentian root, orange peel, sage

NOTES
Copper color. Highly aromatic. Orange, floral, and bitter.

BROVO SPIRITS AMARO

Woodinville, Washington, United States

BroVo's Amaro Project began with $25,000 worth of an experimental rhubarb liqueur that wasn't quite up to snuff. BroVo's Mhairi Voelsgen turned samples over to local bartenders in Seattle as a base for crafting their own amaro. Since then, the Amaro Project has expanded to Chicago, New York, Atlanta, and San Francisco. These regional amari are released annually in limited editions with some of the greatest hits, like Amaro No. 1 (from John Ueding, Seattle: a citrus-rich Gran Classico style sweetened with agave nectar; 30 percent alcohol), No. 4 (from Patrick Haight, Seattle: a floral gateway amaro with citrus and hibiscus possessing a spicy kick from cayenne pepper; 30 percent alcohol), and No. 14 (from Mike Ryan, Chicago: smoky with chocolate, cinnamon, and sarsaparilla; 30 percent alcohol) staying in rotation as their flagship amari.

CALISAYA

Eugene, Oregon, United States

ALCOHOL BY VOLUME
35 percent

KNOWN INGREDIENTS
Agave nectar, calisaya, cinchona bark, bitter orange

NOTES
Copper color. Woodsy, fresh, and spicy with a delicate orange peel bitterness.

Made in small, hand-numbered batches, Calisaya, named after a variety of liqueur made using *Cinchona calisaya* as a bittering agent, started as a homemade amaro experiment from Italian-born chef Andrea Loreto. After 138 test batches, the formula was finalized and released in 2010.

CH AMARO

Chicago, Illinois, United States

ALCOHOL BY VOLUME
40 percent

KNOWN INGREDIENTS
Cocoa nibs, gentian root, grapefruit peel, honey

NOTES
Dark copper color. Bitter with moderate sweetness and smoky notes of rich chocolate.

CH Amaro was born from necessity. While trying to place their CH Vodka at the Chicago bar the Dawson, they couldn't negotiate a well placement; then the bar manager said, "If you make an amaro, I'll sell tons of it." And thus, in 2014, CH Amaro was born. Made using their molasses-rich, unaged CH Rum as a base, it features Illinois ingredients such as cocoa nibs roasted at Ethereal Chocolates in Woodstock, Illinois, and honey from a local beekeeper at Hawk Hill Bee Farm in Marengo. Cofounder and master distiller Tremaine Atkinson notes, "We love experimentation and having a clientele that really understand amaro, so making an amaro was a natural for us."

GOLDEN MOON AMER DIT PICON

Golden, Colorado, United States

ALCOHOL BY VOLUME
39 percent

NOTES
Amber color. Balance of bittersweet citrus, with baking spice notes of cinnamon, molasses, and caramel.

Golden Moon Distillery was founded by Stephen Gould and Karen Knight in 2008 and specializes in herbal liqueurs and spirits inspired by the research on distilling they uncover in their extensive rare-book library, with titles dating back to the 1500s. In the summer of 2013, they released their handcrafted, unfiltered American version of Amer Picon, based on the process and techniques of Gaétan Picon's original 1837 recipe.

HIGH WIRE DISTILLING COMPANY SOUTHERN AMARO

Charleston, South Carolina, United States

I like to think that a conversation I had with Scott Blackwell, of Charleston's High Wire Distilling, over an after-dinner drink during Tales of the Cocktail in New Orleans, played a minor role in the spark that brought his Southern Amaro to life. I was rambling on about the potential of regional American-made amaro, and being enamored with Scott Blackwell and Ann Marshall's Southern-inspired, grain-to-glass bourbon, gin, and limited-edition heirloom releases of watermelon brandy and sugarcane agricole, and said, "Where is our great Southern amaro? You should make an amaro." Blackwell said he'd love to but "didn't have a drop of Italian in his blood." He later told me, "I still have the notes I took on my phone regarding Southern bittering agents. I loved the idea and kept thinking about it. So that's what we did." Two years later, High Wire Distilling's Southern Amaro was born.

They looked to local ingredients for inspiration, like the bitter berries from the yaupon holly that grew on the tree in their front yard; the Dancy tangerine, "the grandfather of all North American tangerines"; Johns Island mint from a local island grower; Charleston tea from Wadmalaw, thirty minutes from their distillery; and local cane syrup. "I love how it fits a true amaro styling in its regionality, much like Italian amari," Blackwell says.

ALCOHOL BY VOLUME
30 percent

KNOWN INGREDIENTS
Black tea, Dancy tangerine, mint, yaupon holly

NOTES
Dark cola color. Floral with strong notes of citrus and malty tea finish.

JEPPSON'S MALÖRT

Auburndale, Florida, United States

Although production of the much-maligned Jeppson's Malört moved to Florida in the 1980s, its bitter reputation was born in Chicago, where it continues to be knocked back by locals and visitors alike, typically in a rite-of-passage dare rather than appreciation. The fact that one is rarely charged for a shot of Malört is not without significance. Area bartenders helped fuel its infamy, and more first-timer "Malört faces" are born every day as they offer variations on the original served on draft, including smoked and barrel-aged. The roots of Jeppson's Malört go back to Carl Jeppson, a Swedish immigrant living in Chicago in the 1880s, who created a bitter formula inspired by the wormwood schnapps of his homeland and sold it by promoting it bar by bar. It caught on with Swedish and Polish bars of the city.

ALCOHOL BY VOLUME
35 percent

KNOWN INGREDIENTS
Wormwood

NOTES
Urinelike hue. Intensely bitter. Astringent and aggressive. Rocket fuel kick.

LO-FI APERITIFS GENTIAN AMARO

Napa, California, United States

This collaboration between E. & J. Gallo Winery and Philadelphia's Quaker City Mercantile, whose owner Steve Grasse is behind Art in the Age spirits and other brands like Hendrick's gin and Sailor Jerry rum, launched in the Bay Area in late 2015 with two vermouth expressions and a gentian-based, all-natural amaro.

ALCOHOL BY VOLUME
16 percent

KNOWN INGREDIENTS
Anise, cinchona bark, ginger, grapefruit, hibiscus, orange peel

NOTES
Port color. Warm, herbaceous notes with pops of floral citrus.

MARGERUM AMARO

Santa Barbara, California, United States

Inspired by his travels through Italy, California winemaker Doug Margerum created the small-batch Margerum Amaro, which he claims is one of the first—if not the first—domestic-made amaros in the United States. A fortified-wine base is infused with aromatics and botanicals, then aged outdoors in oak barrels for at least a year.

ALCOHOL BY VOLUME
23 percent

KNOWN INGREDIENTS
Lemon verbena, marjoram, mint, orange peel, parsley, rosemary, sage, thyme

NOTES
Port color. Mulled wine and baking spices profile slight bitterness.

R. FRANKLIN'S ORIGINAL RECIPE BËSK

Chicago, Illinois, United States

ALCOHOL BY VOLUME
50 percent

KNOWN INGREDIENTS
Anise, elderflower, gentian root, grapefruit peel, juniper berries, star anise, wormwood

NOTES
Yellow chartreuse color. Strong and bitter. Cough syrup–like licorice dominates with notes of grapefruit and anise.

Formulated by Robby Franklin Hayes and brought to life through a collaboration with Chicago's Letherbee Distillers in 2013, this was first only available at the Violet Hour, where Hayes worked. It traveled under the name malört but a certain Chicago-centric spirit of the same name had issues over whether *malört* was considered an exclusive brand name rather than the name of a spirit category of wormwood-based liqueurs (*malört* is the Swedish word for "wormwood").

ST. AGRESTIS AMARO

Brooklyn, New York, United States

ALCOHOL BY VOLUME
30 percent

KNOWN INGREDIENTS
Angelica root, allspice, Cape aloe, cardamom, cinnamon, clove, coriander, dried bitter orange peel, fresh bitter orange peel, gentian, orris root, peppermint, sarsaparilla root, spearmint

NOTES
Root beer color. Soda fountain flavor or sarsaparilla with warm Christmas spices of cinnamon, vanilla, orange, and spearmint.

Brooklyn's first contemporary amaro was born in Gowanus, created by sommeliers Nicholas Finger and Fairlie McCollough, who worked together at Felidia. As happens when one visits Italy for an extended period of time, their enthusiasm for amaro became an obsession upon their return to the States, and they set out to create a regional amaro to call their own. The *St.* part of the name was a nod to the Italian inspiration, while the meaning of *Agrestis* is "of the field" or "of the wild."

They produce just 120 cases a year from a blend of twenty different organic herbs, fruit, spices, barks, and botanicals. After a two- to three-week maceration process, the amaro is aged in whiskey barrels from Red Hook's Van Brunt Stillhouse for an additional one to two months and is left unfiltered. As Finger points out, "The use of whiskey casks adds a very American spin to the Italian classic in terms of flavor profile." Trying to keep all of the botanicals local proved challenging. "Just like with wine, all the botanicals you use are affected by the terroir, and angelica root from Croatia is different than angelica root from upstate New York," Finger continues. "You have to weigh the flavors and quality of the ingredients with the desire to make a local product while making the best product you can. Sometimes we went local, and other times the quality disparity was so drastic that we went with the nondomestic choice. Amaro is all about the balance of not only bitter and sweet but also the different flavors you are using, and getting everything perfected takes a lot of trial and error."

AMARO DELLE SIRENE

Washington, D.C., United States

Francesco Amodeo grew up in Furore on the Amalfi Coast, and after the master sommelier moved to Washington, D.C., he worked at some of the city's top restaurants. Later, in 2012, he launched a line of colorful and inventive liqueurs from his adopted home. In the summer of 2014, he added a signature amaro to his expanding portfolio at Don Ciccio and Figli that was modeled on an Italian amaro called Certosino, which had a brief production run in 1931 in Atrani at a distillery owned by his grandfather, Don Ciccio. "I didn't want to compete with gin, rye, or bourbon makers," explains Amodeo. "I wanted to work with them to make American-made cocktails with American-made ingredients with flavors that weren't really common." Using a four-ounce sample of the original amaro as inspiration, he concocted his signature amaro from thirty roots, barks, and botanicals and aged it for thirty to forty-five days in French oak imported from Marisa Cuomo Winery on the Amalfi Coast. "The level of bitterness makes a major difference," he continues. "I'm not trying to be too sweet—just the right touch of sweetness. This was crafted for connoisseurs of amaro—deep lovers of bitterness. You don't want to drink candy. You want to taste different flavor profiles as you go." Other amari in his portfolio include "5" Cinque Aperitivo, a low-alcohol aperitivo bitter based on a recipe from 1929; Luna Amara Bitter, a golden-colored Italian Bitter of a Turin-style aperitif liqueur from a recipe dating back to 1894; Amaro Donna Rosa, a "happy accident" during the production process that resulted in a citrus- and floral-forward blend that's barrel-aged for three months in French oak; Amaro Don Ferné, Amodeo's take on a domestic, barrel-aged fernet made with mint, cardoon, artichokes, and saffron; and Amaro delle Sirene Edizione Speciale, a limited edition of his house amaro aged in medium-charred new American oak barrels.

ALCOHOL BY VOLUME
29 percent

KNOWN INGREDIENTS
Angelica root, barley, cassia, cinchona bark, chicory, eucalyptus, gentian, licorice root, passionflower, roasted rhubarb root

NOTES
Tobacco color. Dry with heavy notes of anise and warm fruit spices.

TORANI AMER

San Francisco, California, United States

Created by Torani, maker of the ubiquitous flavored syrups stocked at coffee shops, this amaro is meant to fill the gap left by France's Amer Picon, but its availability is limited to California. It's quite affordable at less than $15 a bottle, but the quality of the product is questionable. It lacks the depth of character of Amer Picon.

ALCOHOL BY VOLUME
39 percent

KNOWN INGREDIENTS
Bitter orange peel, cinchona bark, gentian

NOTES
Copper color. Fruity and bittersweet with herbaceous notes of mint.

CHAPTER 3

APERITIVO

COCKTAILS

SALUTE!

One morning in Milan, my friend and traveling companion Ed Anderson and I stopped by Bar Luce, a café designed by American film director Wes Anderson in the Fondazione Prada complex. Every inch of the space felt lovingly art directed in Anderson's quirky, signature style, from the Steve Zissou–themed pinball machine and the handpicked song selections on the jukebox to the adorable young woman who walked through the doors and ordered an espresso still wearing her scooter helmet. Designed in the style of a mid-century Milanese café, there were oversized glass jars filled with pastel-colored Italian candies, a bakery case with rows of elegant pastries, and bottles of amaro standing at attention on the shelves behind the counter.

We ordered four different bitter sodas to try, and Ed took out his camera and went to work taking some shots of the jewel-toned drinks lined up in a row across the mint-green Formica table. An older Italian woman at the next table leaned in to see what we were up to. "Americans, right?" I thought the camera gave us away as tourists but she was more interested in our drink selection. Then, in a fit of comic exasperation, she asked, "Why do you come all the way to Italy to drink cocktails? America has the best cocktails. Everyone knows that."

Matteo Meletti told me his version of the same story: "Italy exports amaro and America sends back new ways for us to use it in cocktails." My bartender friends in the United States told me the same thing. But by the time I left Italy, I had a very different impression: Italy had a lot more to offer the cocktail world than just classic ruby-red aperitivo drinks.

In Italy, the word *aperitivo* refers to both the tradition of before-dinner drinking and socializing as well as the actual drink consumed. Typically, lower-alcohol drinks are consumed to help stimulate the appetite during the transition from the end of the workday to evening (the Latin definition of *aperitivo* and its French version, *aperitif*, is "to open," as in being receptive to an appetizing sensation). Bars often provide gratis snacks like olives, potato chips, crudités, or nuts to hold you over until the next stop.

There are landmark bars and cafés in Italy famous for their roles in aperitivo culture, and naturally we stopped off at Bar Basso in Milan, Caffè Greco in Rome, and Harry's Bar in Venice. In Milan, cocktail bars like Dry and Nottingham Forest presented well-crafted drinks as solid as those offered by any serious bar you'd see in the States. Leonardo and Francesco Vena, the fourth-generation brothers of the Amaro Lucano family, took us on a whirlwind tour of their neighborhood haunts in Milan's Navigli district, with stops—all with serious cocktails—at Rita, Mag Cafè, and Luca e Andrea. We capped things off with bespoke tableside, culinary-inspired drinks at Carlo e Camilla. In Rome, we had front-row seats at the Jerry Thomas Speakeasy, where we met owner Leonardo Leuci and watched a trio of bartenders compose drinks throughout the night with effortless choreography. And in Ascoli Piceno, Fabio Caponi's charming Bar Sestili is the kind of bar I long to return to, or wish I had in my own neighborhood.

On my last day in Rome, I spent far too much time staring at the vast collection of amari lining the floor-to-ceiling shelves in the front corner of Enoteca Costantini. The variety of brands and expressions available would have an American bartender spinning at the possibilities. I was already weighed down with thirteen bottles I had picked up in my travels and there wasn't room for more. I often think of all of those bottles I had to leave behind and hope we'll cross paths someday soon.

In the cocktail recipes in this chapter, you'll find a lineup of classic Italian aperitivo drinks like the Americano, the Garibaldi, and the much-beloved Negroni. Although they're currently in vogue in the bartending community, most amaro-laced cocktails are relatively modern inventions and don't always come packed with the historical pedigree (and sometimes baggage) that comes with so many golden-age cocktails. That being said, a few drinks, like the Hanky Panky and the Boulevardier, will get special recognition in chapter 4, before we turn to contemporary cocktails from bartenders at celebrated bars and restaurants across America (with a few pit stops in Italy and even Taiwan), in addition to some BTP original mixes created by yours truly in chapter 5. And, as things usually tend to happen, we'll wrap things up with some bittersweet shots.

AMERICANO

MAKES 1 DRINK

*1½ ounces
Campari*

*1½ ounces
sweet vermouth*

Soda water

*Garnish: orange
half-wheel or
orange zest*

The Americano, a low-alcohol highball consisting of Campari, sweet vermouth, and soda water, originated as the Milano-Torino—so named because the Campari was from Milan and the sweet vermouth from Turin. The drink was first served at Milan's Caffè Camparino in 1860, but during Prohibition, tourists and American expats added fizzy soda to the mix and it became known as the Americano. It's also the first of what turned out to be many signature drinks ordered, in meticulous detail, in Ian Fleming's 1953 Bond novel, *Casino Royale*.

My favorite Americano had as much to do with the setting in which it was served as the ingredients in the drink itself. I was driving with photographer Ed Anderson from Milan to Friuli on our way to meet the Nonino family, and after hours on the road, we finally reached our lodging for the night. We were staying at Orsone, a bed and breakfast owned by Joe and Lidia Bastianich in Cividale del Friuli. We checked in at the bar and before taking our bags out of the rental car, we took a seat at one of the patio tables overlooking the rolling hills of the vineyards. Simone, our bartender, brought us a round of Americanos ("for the Americanos," he said with a wink), served in rocks glasses with plenty of ice and a long ribbon of orange zest, leaving the bottles on the table for us to admire. Instead of Campari he had used a brand not available in the United States, the cherry-red Riserva Carlo Alberto Bitter Rouge aperitivo, and a caramel-red-colored Mancino Rosso Amaranto vermouth. We sat in silence, sipping our drinks and picking at a bowl of nuts, as those hours on the road faded into a memory.

Build the Campari and sweet vermouth in a highball glass or old-fashioned glass filled with ice. Top off with soda water. Stir and garnish with the orange half-wheel or orange zest.

CAMPARI AND SODA

APEROL SPRITZ

With its bright orange hue, ice-filled balloon serving glass, and signature black straw peeking over the rim, the Aperol spritz is one of the most ubiquitous and well-known aperitivo drinks across Italy. You can find it in bars, restaurants, and cafés from the north to the south. Much sweeter and not as bitter as Campari, it has a low-alcohol content that makes it the perfect vehicle for daytime drinking, especially during the summer months.

Over the past few years, Gruppo Campari, which purchased the Aperol brand in 2003, has worked to make the Aperol spritz catch on with a younger crowd of drinkers with their "Easy as 3, 2, 1" advertising campaign (referring to the drink's signature proportions of Prosecco, Aperol, and soda water). For more on the topic of the category of wine-based, soda-splashed aperitifs, turn to *Spritz: Italy's Most Iconic Aperitivo Cocktail, with Recipes* by my friends Talia Baiocchi and Leslie Pariseau.

MAKES 1 DRINK

3 ounces Prosecco or sparkling wine

2 ounces Aperol

1 ounce soda water

Garnish: orange slice

Build the Prosecco, Aperol, and soda water in a wineglass or double old-fashioned glass filled with ice. Stir and garnish with the orange slice. Serve with a straw.

CAMPARI AND SODA

One of the easiest and most refreshing ways to enjoy Campari is with a splash of soda water on the rocks. The Italians know a thing or two about low-alcohol, premixed aperitivi sold in cute little bottles, and Campari Soda was the first and most recognizable offering in this category. First made available in 1932, the distinctive miniature bottle—modeled on an overturned chalice—was designed by Fortunato Depero, and it remains an iconic calling card for the brand to this day. The bottle contains no label beyond raised lettering spelling out Campari, letting the signature red hue sell itself.

MAKES 1 DRINK

1½ ounces Campari

Soda water

Garnish: orange slice or orange zest

Build the Campari in a highball or double old-fashioned glass filled with ice. Top off with soda water. Stir and garnish with the orange slice or orange zest.

GARIBALDI

MAKES 1 DRINK

*1½ ounces
Campari*

*4 ounces freshly
squeezed orange
juice*

*Garnish: orange
slice*

This cocktail is named after the popular Italian revolutionary Giuseppe Garibaldi, a central figure in the Italian Resurgence (*Risorgimento*), which ultimately led to the country's unification of north and south in 1861. With just two ingredients, the drink itself displays the red Campari from Milan in the north—with a nod to the red shirts worn by Garibaldi and his all-volunteer army of freedom fighters—and oranges from Sicily in the south. Using freshly squeezed orange juice is key here. At his Italian-influenced aperitivo bar Dante in New York's Greenwich Village, Naren Young juices one orange à la minute through a Breville juicer for each drink order, resulting in a finished drink with a frothy, Orange Julius–like finish.

Build the Campari and orange juice in a highball or double old-fashioned glass filled with ice. Stir and garnish with the orange slice.

NEGRONI SBAGLIATO

Milan's venerable Bar Basso opened in 1947, and in 1967, Mirko Stocchetto, a bartender from Venice, took over the bar and started adding cocktails to the menu to compete with the city's larger hotels and cafés. His son Maurizio Stocchetto now runs Bar Basso and you'll still find a menu of "Classic Cocktails from the Old School" behind the bar, including the White Russian, brandy Alexander, Grasshopper, and Gibson, but the Italian cocktail made famous at Basso is the Negroni Sbagliato.

MAKES 1 DRINK

1 ounce Campari

1 ounce sweet vermouth

1 ounce Prosecco or sparkling wine

Garnish: orange slice or orange zest

Sbagliato means "messed up" or "bungled" in Italian, and as the younger Stocchetto tells it, one night in the late 1960s or early 1970s a bartender had accidentally swapped the gin with a bottle of spumante. When his father was making a customer's Negroni (page 107) he reached for the spot on the bar where the gin was always kept but instead added the dry sparkling wine to the mix of Campari and vermouth. "The customer said, 'Let's try it.' And he didn't complain."

When I asked Stocchetto how many Negroni Sbagliatos he served each day, he just sighed and said "too many." They normally serve it in a comically large hand-blown stemmed glass, the kind of fishbowl-sized vessel you're more likely to encounter at a bachelorette party spilling out onto Bourbon Street, but when I ordered one he insisted on making mine in the standard rocks glass. He reminisced about hanging out at the bar as a boy, but he really lit up telling me about his time living in San Francisco in his twenties. His love of the Beats, jazz, and the NHL play-offs remains strong, but he's particularly entertained by the American fast-food advertisements shown during his beloved hockey games. Taking a pause from serving a customer a supersized Sbagliato, he looked at me and smiled in wonder, "At Subway, they'll put guacamole on anything you want!"

Build the Campari, vermouth, and Prosecco in an old-fashioned glass filled with ice. Stir and garnish with the orange slice or orange zest.

CHAPTER 4

SSENTIAL

AMARO COCKTAILS

BOULEVARDIER

MAKES 1 DRINK

1½ ounces bourbon

¾ ounce Campari

*¾ ounce sweet
vermouth*

*Garnish: orange
zest*

Essentially a Negroni made with bourbon instead of gin, the Boulevardier is one of my favorite cocktails. The bourbon mellows the rich, herbal sweetness of the vermouth and Campari with an almost velvety mouthfeel that I've come to crave, and it's a frequently ordered drink that's often in my hand before, during, and after dinner. Its first appearance in print was in 1927 in Harry McElhone's *Barflies and Cocktails*, and it takes its name from the Parisian magazine *Boulevardier*, which was founded by the drink's creator, American expat Erskine Gwynne. The original recipe called for equal parts bourbon, sweet vermouth, and Campari, but most modern bartenders up the amount of bourbon.

Combine the bourbon, Campari, and sweet vermouth in a mixing glass filled with ice. Stir until chilled and strain into a double old-fashioned glass over a large ice cube or into a chilled coupe or cocktail glass. Garnish with the orange zest.

HANKY PANKY

Before Harry Craddock rose to fame as a celebrated bartender and author of *The Savoy Cocktail Book*, from 1903 through 1926 Ada "Coley" Coleman worked at the American Bar at the Savoy Hotel in London, eventually achieving the position of head bartender. Her most famous creation behind the bar was the Hanky Panky, an equal-parts gin–sweet vermouth martini spiked with two dashes of the inky, bitter, herbal liqueur Fernet-Branca. Actor Sir Charles Hawtrey, a regular at the bar, came in and requested something with "a bit of punch in it," and after tasting Coley's creation declared it as "the real hanky-panky!" In *The PDT Cocktail Book*, Jim Meehan offers a tweak of the classic formula, using two ounces gin, one ounce sweet vermouth, and one-quarter ounce Fernet-Branca, resulting in a drier drink. Give both versions a spin to determine which one agrees with your palate.

....

Combine the gin, sweet vermouth, and Fernet-Branca in a mixing glass filled with ice. Stir until chilled and strain into a chilled coupe or cocktail glass. Garnish with the orange zest.

MAKES 1 DRINK

1½ ounces gin

1½ ounces sweet vermouth

2 dashes Fernet-Branca

Garnish: orange zest

JUNGLE BIRD

MAKES 1 DRINK

1½ ounces blackstrap rum

1½ ounces freshly squeezed pineapple juice

¾ ounce Campari

½ ounce freshly squeezed lime juice

½ ounce simple syrup (page 118)

Garnish: pineapple chunk and/or pineapple leaf

I had my first Jungle Bird, fittingly enough, at the Chicago tiki mecca Three Dots and a Dash. I was meeting drinks writer and author Robert Simonson, and when he picks the spot to meet for cocktails, you know you're in good hands. He suggested I order the Jungle Bird, one of the few tiki drinks to feature amaro—in this case, Campari. I've been back to Three Dots and a Dash for more of those, but I had a less tricked-out version at Seattle's Rob Roy that really sold me on the drink, which was originally created at the Aviary bar at the Kuala Lumpur Hilton around 1979. Though the Jungle Bird was listed in the 1989 *New American Bartender's Guide* by John J. Poister, it wasn't until 2002 that Jeff Berry's *Beachbum Berry's Intoxica!* made it a bartender favorite with a cult following that rivals the Negroni. New York bartender Giuseppe Gonzalez substituted molasses-rich blackstrap rum for the dark rum of the original, and that's the version that lives on today.

Combine all the ingredients except the garnish in a cocktail shaker filled with ice. Shake until chilled and strain into a double old-fashioned glass over a large ice cube. Garnish with the pineapple chunk or leaf (or both).

NEGRONI

In his book *The Negroni*, Gary Regan takes a fascinating tour of the history and mystery of this elegant and sometimes controversial drink. The origin story is still up for debate, but after weighing recent updates uncovered by drinks historian David Wondrich, Regan is "absolutely convinced" that there was indeed a Count Camillo Negroni, who, when he requested gin in place of soda water in his Americano at Caffè Casoni in Florence, Italy, gave birth to his namesake cocktail.

I struggled with whether or not this drink belongs here or the Aperitivo Cocktail section—but ultimately decided that the assertive presence of gin takes it out of the lower-alcohol aperitivo realm. (That having been said, don't let me tell you when to enjoy your Negroni.)

This ruby-red, equal-parts cocktail of gin, Campari, and sweet vermouth has gone on to become one of the most celebrated, and fetishized, drinks of our time. Variations, with and without Campari, abound, and it has taken on new life in the form of bottled and barrel-aged versions. For the past few years in June, the global charity event Negroni Week has consumed bartenders and cocktail aficionados alike with a passion for this bittersweet superstar of the cocktail world.

MAKES 1 DRINK

1 ounce gin

1 ounce Campari

1 ounce sweet vermouth

Garnish: orange zest

....

Build the gin, Campari, and sweet vermouth in an old-fashioned glass filled with ice. Stir and garnish with the orange zest.

Or combine the gin, Campari, and sweet vermouth in a mixing glass filled with ice. Stir until chilled and strain into a rocks glass filled with ice or over a large ice cube, or into a chilled coupe or cocktail glass. Garnish with the orange zest.

OLD PAL

MAKES 1 DRINK

1½ ounces rye whiskey

¾ ounce Campari

¾ ounce dry vermouth

Garnish: lemon zest

Like many drinks with dueling and dubious origin stories, the Old Pal has evolved over the years. There is debate as to whether it should be made with dry French or sweet Italian vermouth, but the former dry version is what you'll likely receive if you order one at a bar. (Sub in sweet vermouth, and you have something similar to a Boulevardier.) In his book, *The Negroni*, Gary Regan recommends, "Whatever type of vermouth you use, this cocktail works best with a good straight rye; try using Michter's, Rittenhouse 100, or Sazerac."

Combine the rye, Campari, and dry vermouth in a mixing glass filled with ice. Stir until chilled and strain into a chilled coupe or cocktail glass. Garnish with the lemon zest.

TORONTO

MAKES 1 DRINK

2 ounces rye or Canadian whiskey

¼ ounce Fernet-Branca

¼ ounce Demerara syrup (see page 118)

2 dashes Angostura bitters

Garnish: orange twist

A relative from the north to America's old-fashioned cocktail, the Fernet-kissed Toronto remains one of my favorite, spirit-forward cool-weather cocktails. David A. Embury's 1948 book *The Fine Art of Mixing Drinks* contains the printed recipe most people reference, but it's been pointed out that Robert Vermiere's *Cocktails: How to Mix Them* from 1922 contains a "Fernet Cocktail" of similar composition with the boast that "this cocktail is much appreciated by the Canadians of Toronto."

Combine all the ingredients except the garnish in a mixing glass filled with ice. Stir until chilled and strain into a chilled coupe or cocktail glass. Garnish with the orange twist.

TORONTO

CHAPTER 5

MODERN

AMARO COCKTAILS

ALPINE SLIDE

MAKES I DRINK

1 ounce Amaro Bràulio

1 ounce Byrrh Grand Quinquina

½ ounce Dolin Blanc vermouth

Scant ½ ounce Champagne acid (see Note)

2½ ounces soda water

Since it opened in January 2012, the menu at Booker and Dax, Dave Arnold's science-minded drinks den connected to Momofuku Ssäm Bar in Manhattan's East Village, has had a section dedicated to carbonated drinks. Arnold understands that most home kitchens aren't outfitted with custom-built carbonation rigs, though you can learn plenty on the topic in his award-winning book *Liquid Intelligence*. The at-home bartender can achieve domestic-level carbonation by employing some seltzer and a little Champagne acid.

Booker and Dax bartender Jack Schramm's "love of all things bubbly and bitter" and his desire to create a cold-weather drink with the spirit of a summertime spritz inspired the Alpine Slide. And when it comes to all things Alpine, Bràulio, hailing from Bormio in the Italian Alps, is the après-ski amaro you want to put into service. This herbaceous, oak barrel–aged blend hits you like a walk through a snowy forest. And the addition of the lightly bitter, aromatic French aperitif wine Byrrh, rounded out with a bit of brightness from dry vermouth, makes this the black diamond of bitter, wintertime spritzes.

Combine the Amaro Bràulio, Byrrh, vermouth, and Champagne acid in a mixing glass filled with ice and stir very quickly—just enough to chill the solution without overdiluting the mixture, which will lower the level of carbonation. (In a best-case scenario, chill all of the liquor bottles in the fridge or briefly in the freezer and mix together without ice before topping the drink with seltzer.) Pour into a chilled Champagne flute and top with soda water.

NOTE To make the Champagne acid, dissolve 3 grams lactic acid and 3 grams tartaric acid in 9 milliliters of water. Acid powders are available from specialty food stores or online retailers like Amazon. If you're eager to dive in and you want to make the drink without Champagne acid, it will still work, but increase the vermouth to ¾ ounce.

ALPINE SOUR

MAKES 1 DRINK

1 ounce Asbach Uralt German brandy

1 ounce orgeat, preferably Orgeat Works T'Orgeat toasted almond syrup

1 ounce freshly squeezed lemon juice

1 bottle Underberg

Garnish: freshly grated nutmeg

Damon Boelte now runs his own bar, Grand Army, in Brooklyn's Boerum Hill, but his storied tenure as bar director at Prime Meats is where he became known for his love of Underberg (see page 66), the German herbal digestive bitters sold in single-serve 20-millilter bottles. He started playing around, putting a couple of drops of Underberg in a Manhattan instead of Angostura, and then it hit him. "I had a dream one night—it's insane, I get a lot of work done when I sleep." In a spirited dream rivaling one of *Twin Peaks'* Special Agent Dale Cooper's vision quests, Boelte saw the Trinidad Sour (a modern classic created by New York bartender Giuseppe Gonzalez, which calls for a full ounce of Angostura bitters) and swapped in a whole bottle of Underberg in place of the Angostura. Underberg is meant to be consumed on its own and not dispatched as a potent cocktail ingredient, but if you do want to add it to your backbar, heed Boelte's parting advice: "Underberg is a funny thing, man. When making a cocktail, get greedy. Don't just put a dash in there, put in the whole bottle." Bitter words to live by, indeed.

....

Combine all the ingredients except the garnish in a cocktail shaker filled with ice. Shake until chilled and strain into a chilled coupe or cocktail glass. Garnish with the freshly grated nutmeg.

AMARO AMANTÉ

I first met Taylor Parsons when he was at Osteria Mozza and he's now the general manager and beverage director at Los Angeles restaurant République. Though we can't confirm it, he suspects I may be a long-lost relative. I should be so lucky. He connected me with République's bar program director, Shawn Lickliter, who shared this aperitif for whiskey lovers. "I chose Old Overholt rye because the fresh apple, cinnamon, and ginger palate play nice with Abano's cinnamon, pine, and chocolate notes. This cocktail has a cool tiki feel to it but drinks like an aperitif."

....

Combine all the ingredients except the garnish in a cocktail shaker filled with ice. Shake until chilled and strain into a collins glass filled with ice. Garnish with the lemon zest.

MAKES 1 DRINK

1 ounce Old Overholt rye whiskey

1 ounce Luxardo Amaro Abano

¾ ounce freshly squeezed pineapple juice

¾ ounce freshly squeezed lemon juice

½ ounce Evaporated Cane Sugar Syrup (recipe follows)

Garnish: lemon zest

EVAPORATED CANE SUGAR SYRUP

In a medium saucepan over medium heat, bring the sugar and water to a simmer, stirring the mixture occasionally to dissolve the sugar. At the first crack of a boil, remove from the heat. Let cool completely, then store the syrup in a glass jar with a lid. The syrup will keep in the refrigerator for up to a month.

MAKES 1½ CUPS

1 cup water

1 cup raw cane sugar

AMARO SOUR

Mixing up my boozy and sugary analogies, amaro and bourbon comes close to topping the classic pairing of peanut butter and chocolate. It isn't surprising that many American bartenders embracing the use of amaro in cocktails will reach for a classic American spirit like bourbon to pair it with. The amaro sour template allows you to mix and match your bourbon with amaro. I recommend complementing the bourbon with a lighter, user-friendly, gateway amaro like Amaro Lucano, Luxardo Amaro Abano, or Averna rather than going to the dark end of the bracingly medicinal spectrum. Portland bartender Jeffrey Morgenthaler makes the self-proclaimed "best amaretto sour in the world," and I—along with legions of bartenders—agree with him. It's his updated specs that are on display here, swapping the amaretto for amaro. I like this served with a frothy head on the rocks, but you can also try it served up in a chilled coupe glass.

MAKES 1 DRINK

1½ ounces amaro

¾ ounce bourbon

1 ounce freshly squeezed lemon juice

¼ ounce simple syrup (page 118)

1 egg white

Garnish: lemon zest and cocktail cherry

....

Combine all the ingredients except the garnish in a cocktail shaker and dry shake (without ice) for at least 10 seconds to fully incorporate the egg white. Add ice and continue shaking until chilled and strain into a double old-fashioned glass filled with ice. Garnish with the lemon zest and cocktail cherry.

SIMPLE SYRUP

MAKES 1½ CUPS

1 cup sugar

1 cup water

In a medium saucepan over medium heat, bring the sugar and water to a simmer, stirring the mixture occasionally to dissolve the sugar. At the first crack of a boil, remove from the heat. Let cool completely, then store the syrup in a glass jar with a lid. The syrup will keep in the refrigerator for up to a month.

DEMERARA SYRUP

1 cup Demerara or turbinado sugar

1 cup water

To make Demerara Syrup, follow the same recipe as above but use Demerara or turbinado sugar.

CITRUS ZESTS, TWISTS, AND GARNISHES

Many of the drink recipes that follow instruct you to "garnish with a twist." Unless otherwise noted, a simple, thin strip of zest cut from the fruit with a vegetable peeler or knife will do. Some drinks warrant a thick "zest," which, as described, is simply a larger swath of zest peeled from the fruit—a Y-peeler comes in handy for this. Feel free to improvise with the size or design of your citrus zests, but I encourage you to take cues from your serving glass. A thinner strip of curled zest seems at home peeking over a tall Champagne flute, while a thick orange zest is more appropriate for a hefty double old-fashioned glass.

As for other citrus garnishes, a slice and wedge are one and the same, a wheel is a whole circle of citrus slice, and a half-wheel is the the former but cut in half.

Don't forget that twists are there for more than decoration. Before serving, twist your garnish over the drink to express the essential oils from the citrus peel, then rub it around the rim of the glass before placing it in, or on, the glass.

For drinks that call for a flamed orange zest, it's not as scary as it sounds. Using a paring knife, cut a good-sized oval of zest from an orange. Hold it over the glass between your thumb and index finger. With your other hand, light a match and then place it between the orange zest and the glass. Slowly press the edges of the zest together, folding it in half, to express the citrus oils, which will ignite in little sparks over the drink.

When a drink calls for a "cocktail cherry," please avoid any artificially colored neon-red so-called Maraschino versions soaking in artificial syrup and instead use a quality brand of cherries like those from Luxardo, Amarena cherries from Fabbri, or your own homemade bourbon or brandied cherries.

THE ART OF THE CHOKE/ KYLE'S AFTER PORK DIGESTIF

Under "House Favorites" on the dessert menu at the Publican restaurant in Chicago, you'll find something called Kyle's After Pork Digestif. I first tried this end-of-meal closer when a glass was produced after I had helped take down a family-sized platter of their famous ham chop in hay at a Publican pop-up at Momofuku Ssäm Bar in New York. The server explained that they used a house-made amaro at the restaurant, which made me eager to learn more.

Kyle, it turns out, is Kyle Davidson, head bartender at Publican's sister restaurant, Blackbird. He told me that his namesake drink was born in 2008, when he was working at both the Violet Hour and the Publican. It's origin story begins with a Cynar-based cocktail he created called The Art of the Choke, which was later published in the books *Rogue Cocktails* and *Beta Cocktails* by Kirk Estopinal and Maksym Pazuniak. When guests at the Publican were over-ordering, he'd suggest this drink to help them push through to the end. Then he found the drink made more of a statement with diners when he batched the drink and brought it to the table in a glass bottle with shot glasses. This method of service proved popular enough that The Art of the Choke cocktail morphed into the large-format service Kyle's After Pork Digestif.

THE ART OF THE CHOKE

Place the mint in a mixing glass and muddle until lightly bruised. Add the Cynar, rum, Chartreuse, Demerara syrup, lime juice, and bitters and fill with ice. Stir until chilled and strain into an old-fashioned glass filled with ice. Garnish with the remaining mint sprig.

MAKES 1 DRINK

2 mint sprigs

1 ounce Cynar

1 ounce white rum, preferably Flor de Caña or Ron Botran

¼ ounce green Chartreuse

1/8 ounce Demerara syrup (see page 118)

1/8 ounce freshly squeezed lime juice

1 dash Angostura bitters

Garnish: mint sprig

KYLE'S AFTER PORK DIGESTIF

Combine all of the ingredients except the mint in a large glass jar or bottle with a lid. Place the mint in a mixing glass or cocktail shaker and muddle until lightly bruised. Add the mint to the batched alcohol and steep for 5 minutes, then remove and discard. Store in the refrigerator for up to a week. To serve, pour about 2 ounces into a chilled old-fashioned or bistro glass.

MAKES 1 BATCH OF APPROXIMATELY 20 SERVINGS

2 cups Cynar

2 cups white rum, preferably Flor de Caña or Ron Botran

4½ ounces green Chartreuse

1½ ounces Demerara syrup (see page 118)

1¼ ounces freshly squeezed lime juice

2½ ounces cool filtered water

5 mint sprigs

AVERNA SMASH

MAKES I DRINK

½ teaspoon high-quality walnut oil

1 brandied cherry

1 orange slice

2 ounces bourbon, preferably Knob Creek

1 ounce Averna

Fever-Tree bitter lemon soda

Garnish: orange zest and cocktail cherry

Seattle chef Jason Stratton has since moved on from the Italian restaurant Spinasse and its modern Italian-style aperitivo bar, Artusi, but a cocktail he created called the Averna Smash lives on. Stratton told me he has long been drawn to bitter flavors and the Italian ritual of amaro served after a meal, but he's a strong believer that "using amaro in a cocktail is a better way of helping people understand it than offering a flight of amari at the end of dinner." And about that walnut oil? A culinary touch from a chef playing around behind the bar to "make if feel more like food."

Combine the walnut oil, brandied cherry, and orange slice in a cocktail shaker and gently muddle until the fruit is just broken up. Add the bourbon and Averna and fill with ice. Shake until chilled and double-strain into a double old-fashioned glass filled with ice. Top off with the bitter lemon soda. Garnish with the orange zest and cocktail cherry.

BARTENDER ON ACID

MAKES I DRINK

1¼ ounces Kalani coconut rum liqueur

¾ ounce Amaro Nardini

¼ ounce El Dorado cask-aged 3-year Demerara rum

¼ ounce green Chartreuse

¼ ounce freshly squeezed lime juice

¾ ounce freshly squeezed pineapple juice

Garnish: pineapple leaf

Brooklyn bartender Garret Richard's last shift at my local, Prime Meats, happened to coincide with its first ever '70s Night. A rotating disco ball splashed a moody rainbow of colors around the bar as Curtis Mayfield's "Move on Up" and Harry Nilsson's "Jump into the Fire" pounded through the speakers. Men wore full-length Joe Namath–style fur coats, the bar served updated spins on the Grasshopper and Alabama Slammer, and instead of the regular dinner menu, the kitchen served bespoke TV dinners (though my TV dinners from that era never came with a foie gras entrée).

The next day, I was somehow able to see through my fern bar–sized hangover to ask Richard for the recipe for one of my favorite featured drinks of the night, the Bartender on Acid. Mashing together two of his favorite things—tiki ephemera and liquor ads from the 1970s—he was aiming for a tropical cocktail that riffed on the 1970s-era drinks the Swampwater (green Chartreuse, pineapple and lime juices) and Surfer on Acid (Jägermeister, Malibu coconut rum, pineapple juice). The more sophisticated Amaro Nardini adds to the complex, herbal base ingredients along with fresh juices, and a little dry, Cuban-style rum adds structure (a tip he picked up from New Orleans tiki bar Latitude 29). "The cocktail is the drink equivalent of a Tarantino film, borrowing the best the '70s had to offer and then making it better," says Richard.

....

Combine all the ingredients except the garnish in a cocktail shaker filled with ice. Shake until chilled and strain into an old-fashioned glass filled with ice. Garnish with the pineapple leaf.

BITTER GIUSEPPE

"I think my best cocktails are typically dealer's choice with a little bit of guidelines," says Chicago bartender Stephen Cole. He was part of the opening team of the celebrated bar the Violet Hour and created the Bitter Giuseppe soon after its opening in 2007. "This was the beginning of my career bartending, so a lot of my cocktails were built in steps," Cole explains. Step one, sparked by a conversation with Chicago chef Giuseppe Tentori, was to create his take on a Cynar Manhattan. Sweet vermouth and Cynar proved too sweet for his tastes, but the bright acidity from the addition of fresh lemon juice did the trick.

The recipe below is for the classic; however, for a 2.0 version of Cole's Bitter Giuseppe, follow New Orleans bartender Kirk Estopinal's lead: his Search for Delicious uses ¾ ounce of Punt e Mes in place of the Carpano Antica Formula, plus two pinches of kosher salt to counterbalance the bitterness. Finally, he expresses five lemon twists over the finished drink and leaves one behind for garnish.

....

Combine the Cynar, vermouth, lemon juice, and bitters in a mixing glass filled with ice. Stir until chilled and strain into a double old-fashioned glass over a large ice cube. Garnish with the lemon zest.

MAKES I DRINK

2 ounces Cynar

1 ounce Carpano Antica Formula sweet vermouth

¼ ounce freshly squeezed lemon juice

6 dashes Regans' Orange Bitters No. 6

Garnish: lemon zest

THE BITTER SWAGGER

MAKES I DRINK

*1¼ ounces
Amaro Nardini*

¾ ounce pisco

*¼ ounce Cocchi
Americano*

*½ ounce freshly
squeezed lemon
juice*

1 egg white

For the past few years I've been making an annual trip down to Memphis and, without fail, I bookend my visit with stops at Hog and Hominy to see my friends, chefs Andy Ticer and Mike Hudman. They serve up some of my favorite Southern-inspired takes on Italian fare, including an insane mortadella hot dog and the Lil Red Ed, a pizza topped with speck, spicy peppers, fontina cheese, tomato sauce, and olives named after our mutual friend Ed Anderson, who also photographed the guys' cookbook, *Collards and Carbonara.*

Nick Talarico oversees the front of the house and the beverage program for their ever-expanding restaurants and also makes a mean old-fashioned, which he doctors with house-made Shiftless Hog orange bitters. I always love geeking out over cocktails and trying new local spirits and beers with Talarico and he kindly shared the story of the Bitter Swagger with me, a cocktail on the menu at Andrew Michael Italian Kitchen, just across the street from Hog and Hominy. "We had a comedian come in after his show downtown late one Saturday night, and he and I talked for a bit about Nardini amaro. He ended up leaving with a bottle from our stock to take with him on his tour and after he left." That encounter inspired Nick to add a drink on the menu that focused on amaro as a base spirit, and a pisco sour template did the trick. "It's a total cocktail nerd drink—amaro, pisco, and egg whites don't necessarily sell themselves—but that's the fun of having a few cocktail lists where you can hide your nerdiest drinks," Talarico says.

Combine all the ingredients in a cocktail shaker and dry shake (without ice) for at least 10 seconds to fully incorporate the egg white. Add ice and continue shaking until chilled and then double-strain into a chilled coupe or cocktail glass.

BJÓRN SUPREMACY

MAKES 1 DRINK

*1½ ounces
overproof rye
whiskey*

*½ ounce Bäska
Snaps med Malört*

*½ ounce Briottet
crème de peche*

*2 dashes Dr. Adam
Elmegirab's Boker's
Bitters*

I first met Dennis Gobis when he was tending bar at Drink.Well in Austin, and since then he's gone on to open his own place in town called the Roosevelt Room. The Bjórn Supremacy was the first (of several) cocktails he made for me that night. The name is a play on the Robert Ludlum thriller and, Gobis adds, "seemed fitting for a cocktail accented with a Scandinavian spirit." He was aiming for a stirred whiskey cocktail that was light but had depth, and the Bäska Snaps, which had just become available in Texas that summer, did the trick. "The pairing of the peach and the wormwood, licorice, and citrus notes was a perfect play off the overproof rye whiskey and lent just enough sweetness to balance out the drink." For me, it remains unclear if the Bjórn Supremacy awoke me from my own Jason Bourne–like state of amnesia or played a role in bringing it on. Either way, I can't remember.

....

Combine all the ingredients in a cocktail shaker filled with ice. Shake until chilled and strain into a chilled coupe or cocktail glass.

"I don't like using an amaro in a cocktail just for the sake of using an amaro. I think we need to have a profound understanding of the spirit category before we start mixing it. Before an amaro cocktail goes on a menu, everyone at that bar should know everything there is to know about the spirit on its own first, from the base spirit to the botanicals, bittering agents, added sugars, and aging. Once we can appreciate the spirit by itself, then we can best find how to showcase it in cocktail form."

—DENNIS GOBIS
The Roosevelt Room, Austin, Texas

BLACK MANHATTAN

Like the Negroni, the template for the Manhattan cocktail (bourbon or rye, sweet vermouth, bitters) serves as a launching pad for so many variations on a theme. The Black Manhattan, which originated at Bourbon and Branch in San Francisco in 2007, swaps in Averna for the traditional sweet vermouth, dialing up both the sweet and the bitter in the equation. Made in Caltanissetta, Sicily, since 1868, Averna brings a spicy, herbal sweetness with a bit of caramel and honey notes. Other gateway amaros like Ramazzotti, Zucca, or Cynar could also step up here and offer their own subtle spins on the drink.

MAKES 1 DRINK

2 ounces bourbon

1 ounce Averna

1 dash Angostura bitters

1 dash orange bitters

Garnish: cocktail cherry

Combine all the ingredients except the garnish in a mixing glass filled with ice. Stir until chilled and strain into a chilled coupe or cocktail glass. Garnish with the cocktail cherry.

BOSS COLADA

Before New Orleans's Cane and Table opened for business, managing partner and bartender Nick Detrich was working on a sour that combined the herbal, Alpine liqueur génépi and pineapple juice for a pop-up preview of upcoming drinks that would eventually make their way into rotation beyond the opening menu. Eventually, Bäska Snaps—a Nordic-style wormwood-based liqueur created by Avery and Janet Glasser, known worldwide for their line of Bittermens cocktail bitters—was subbed in for the génépi, and Detrich had "a drink that was rich and tropical, but dried out considerably by the wormwood, licorice, and other citrus." It fit in with the "ideology" of Cane and Table so well that it was scrapped for the preview and added to the debut menu, where it has remained ever since. Detrich advises serving the Bäska Snaps straight from the refrigerator, saying, "The viscosity increases, and some of the richer chocolate tones become more pronounced."

MAKES 1 DRINK

1 ounce Bäska Snaps med Malört

½ ounce Banks 7 Golden Age rum

1½ ounces freshly squeezed pineapple juice

½ ounce freshly squeezed lime juice

½ ounce orgeat

3 dashes Peychaud's Bitters

Garnish: lime wheel

Combine all the ingredients except the Peychaud's Bitters and garnish in a cocktail shaker filled with ice. Shake until chilled (Detrich calls for 20 shakes) and double-strain into a footed pilsner glass filled with pebble ice (or crushed ice). Add more pebble (or crushed) ice to the top of the glass and coat with the Peychaud's Bitters. Garnish with the lime wheel.

"When incorporating amari as a component into cocktails, more often than not, you will find bartenders using it as a substitution for vermouth. This can yield interesting results, but I've found that citrus and salts can also offer a lot of pleasant surprises. The citrus can help to disperse the various essential oils and flavor extracts contained in the amaro, and with a lower density of those compounds, it becomes easier for the receptors in the mouth to process those flavors. The salt also has the effect of blocking the receptors in the tongue (scrambling the signal to the brain, really) and allowing more complex flavors of the amaro to be perceived."

—NICK DETRICH
Cane and Table, New Orleans, Louisiana

THE BRAVE

MAKES I DRINK

1 ounce Del Maguey Chichicapa mezcal

1 ounce 7 Leguas blanco tequila

½ ounce Averna

1 barspoon Royal Combier, Grand Marnier, or another curaçao

3 mists Angostura bitters

Garnish: flamed orange zest (page 118)

A drink that took Anvil Bar and Refuge owner Bobby Heugel a year to perfect, the Brave remains the bar's house cocktail—it hasn't come off the menu since day one. Hard to believe for a room-temperature drink that's neither shaken nor stirred—just swirled. Bobby told me: "I love drinking both agave spirits and amaro at room temperature, and amaros are among the few that I can think of that can stand up to mezcal. This cocktail is the perfect cocktail to end the evening, but with amaro and agave straightforward, it is only for the brave."

....

In a wineglass, combine the mezcal, tequila, Averna, and curaçao and swirl together. Using an atomizer or an olive oil mister, mist 3 small pumps of bitters on the insides of the glass above the cocktail. Garnish with a flamed orange zest, rested on the rim of the wineglass.

THE BRUNCH BOX

Rebekah Graham, formerly Publican's wine and beer coordinator, collaborated on this riff on the Lunch Box—a glass of beer and orange juice with a dropped shot of amaretto—with former Publican bar manager Matt Poli. Graham became hip to the Lunch Box when a customer ordered a round when she was tending bar at the Pump Room in 2006. Inspired by the endless themes of vintage lunch boxes, she went to work: "We made a Strawberry Shortcake Lunch Box with strawberry Stoli, pineapple juice, and hard apple cider; a Dukes of Hazzard Lunch Box with Southern Comfort, iced tea, and Budweiser; even a Star Wars Lunch Box with blue curaçao, grape juice, and Belgian brown ale. Needless to say, they were all, basically, just gross." But the eureka moment came later, when she subbed in Amaro Montenegro for the amaretto. Poli adds, "Montenegro has a bit of an orange peel character, which is perfect for breakfast and plays with grapefruit nicely."

MAKES 1 DRINK

1 ounce Amaro Montenegro

1 ounce freshly squeezed grapefruit juice, chilled

5 ounces beer, preferably lager, chilled

Build the Amaro Montenegro and grapefruit juice in a chilled collins glass. Top off with beer.

CANTINA BAND

CANTINA BAND

Because sometimes Figrin D'an and the Modal Nodes just isn't a catchy enough name for a cocktail. With apologies to all of the non–*Star Wars* fans out there, the alien playing the toe-tapping number on kloo horn with his fellow Bith bandmates at the Mos Eisley Cantina lives on in spirit in the Cantina Band, from the restaurant Perla in Greenwich Village. This Fernet-Branca-spiked drink is a boozy, bitter summer cooler that will quench the thirst of a sun-scorched Tatooine moisture farmer, or a New Yorker on a humid August afternoon.

MAKES 1 DRINK

1½ ounces Fernet-Branca

½ ounce gin

¾ ounce simple syrup (page 118)

3 cucumber slices

Ginger beer

Garnish: cucumber slice or cucumber ribbon

....

Combine the Fernet-Branca, gin, simple syrup, and cucumber slices in a cocktail shaker filled with ice. Shake until chilled and strain into a collins glass filled with ice. Top off with ginger beer. Garnish with the cucumber slice or cucumber ribbon.

CAPPELLETTI SPRITZ

It's easy to fall in love with the restaurant Franny's in Prospect Heights, Brooklyn. Even when it moved down the block to a bigger space, this Flatbush Avenue institution still held on to its charm and intimacy. Beyond the artfully blistered pizzas (their clam pie is my go-to order), you'll find a deep bench of amari, including several they make in-house and offer in tasting flights. Rolling solo at the bar over the years, I've gotten to know bartender Colin Clarke, who is always eager to show me the new bottles they've brought in. When they started carrying the tangy white wine–based Cappelletti Vino Aperitivo, I got in the habit of kicking things off with a Cappelletti spritz. I always ask for it in a rocks glass, but when I order it at other restaurants it never quite tastes as good as Clarke's. He's such a nice guy that all I really had to do was ask him for the recipe, which I'm now sharing with you.

MAKES 1 DRINK

1½ ounces Cappelletti Vino Aperitivo

½ ounce freshly squeezed lemon juice

¼ ounce simple syrup (page 118)

Prosecco

Garnish: orange zest

....

Build the Cappelletti, lemon juice, and simple syrup in an old-fashioned glass filled with ice. Top off with Prosecco and stir. Garnish with the orange zest.

CARDINAL

MAKES 1 DRINK

1 ounce Tanqueray No. 10 gin

¾ ounce Casoni 1814 Aperitivo

½ ounce Vermouth del Professore Rosso

½ ounce freshly squeezed pink grapefruit juice

¼ ounce fresh squeezed lemon juice

1 barspoon Contratto Fernet

This refreshing scarlet-hued aperitif owes its color to the combination of pink grapefruit and Casoni 1814 Aperitivo, and it made its debut on the spring 2014 menu at the popular East Village bar PDT. It also calls for the barrel-aged Vermouth del Professore Rosso, a collaboration between Antica Distilleria Quaglia in Mazzè outside of Turin and the Jerry Thomas Speakeasy in Rome. PDT general manager and head bartender Jeff Bell says the finished drink should "resemble a cardinal's cassock."

Combine all the ingredients except the fernet in a cocktail shaker filled with ice. Shake until chilled and strain into a chilled coupe or cocktail glass rinsed with the Contratto Fernet.

CARROLL GARDENS

MAKES 1 DRINK

2 ounces rye whiskey, preferably Rittenhouse

½ ounce Amaro Nardini

½ ounce Punt e Mes

1 scant barspoon Luxardo maraschino liqueur

Lemon zest

I have a special place in my heart for Joaquín Simó's signature Carroll Gardens cocktail, and not just because I reside in the Brooklyn neighborhood it's named after. Simó, too, was living in Carroll Gardens when he came up with the drink, a hat tip to Enzo Errico's Red Hook cocktail, which has become a modern classic and spawned a family tree of geographically named drinks celebrating the borough, including the Greenpoint, Bushwick, and Cobble Hill. Simó, a partner in the Lower East Side bar Pouring Ribbons, explains, "My contribution to this family of brown-and-stirred cousins nods to the Italian-American roots of Carroll Gardens. There are still tons of tiny little social clubs, Italian delis, and butchers and bakers, and more Madonna with Child statues in the front-facing lawns of the brownstones than you can shake a stick at." Simó starts with a base spirit of classic American rye but turns to Italy for the modifiers. A whisper of maraschino offers suggestions of stone fruit and marzipan," he says.

Combine the rye, Nardini, Punt e Mes, and maraschino in a mixing glass filled with ice. Stir until chilled and strain into a chilled coupe or cocktail glass. Express the lemon zest over the surface of the drink and discard.

THE CHIPILEÑOS

Being a creature of habit comes into play when I travel, and whenever I'm in New Orleans, locals are quick to point out that there are other restaurants in the city besides Cochon and Cochon Butcher.

Thankfully, delicious cocktails are served at both locations and the Chipileños is another restaurant drink that takes inspiration from the kitchen. Bar manager Denise Spain says of working with chef de cuisine Matt Woodall: "One of my favorite aspects of the bar at Cochon is the ability to collaborate with our phenomenal chefs on different projects, sometimes if even by mistake, as was the case with this cocktail. Our chefs were playing around with kumquats picked from the tree in my front yard, believe it or not, but the project didn't quite go as planned. We turned the pickled kumquats into an amazing kumquat syrup and ran away with the inspiration." This led them to a drink that was layered and complex and ultimately a tribute to Chipilo, a town in Puebla, Mexico, founded by immigrants from Veneto, Italy. "We found it the perfect homage to the importance of amaro to the Italian palate, and agave spirit to the Mexican."

Sal de gussano ("worm salt") is a blend of sea salt, chile peppers, and dried Maguey worms that is often served as a condiment alongside tequila, mezcal, and salsas in Mexico. It can be purchased online on Amazon or The Meadow. If you can't find it, a pinch of sea salt and chili powder can serve as a not-so-authentic substitute.

MAKES 1 DRINK

1½ ounces Mezcal Vago Elote

¾ ounce Amaro Lucano

¾ ounce Pickled Kumquat Syrup (recipe follows)

Pinch of sal de gusano

Combine all the ingredients in a cocktail shaker filled with ice. Shake until chilled and strain into a double old-fashioned glass filled with ice.

PICKLED KUMQUAT SYRUP

Kumquats are typically in season along with other winter citrus from January through March. Slice the kumquats in half. Combine the halved kumquats, vinegar, and sugar in a medium saucepan over medium heat. Bring to a boil, stirring occassinally, then turn down the heat slightly. Allow the syrup to simmer for 10 to 15 minutes, until the kumquats are tender and the liquid becomes syrupy. Remove from the heat. Let cool completely, then strain into a glass jar with a lid. The kumquat syrup will keep in the refrigerator for up to a month.

MAKES APPROXIMATELY 2½ CUPS

8 ounces kumquats

2 cups white vinegar

1 cup sugar

CHOKE AND SMOKE

MAKES I DRINK

1½ ounces Talisker 10-year single-malt scotch whisky

1½ ounces Cynar

1 barspoon Brown Sugar Cordial (recipe follows)

Pinch of kosher salt

3 orange zests

Garnish: orange zest

The Smoking Gun, a Fernet-Branca and scotch cocktail from Idaho bartender Mark Allen, served as the inspiration for the Choke and Smoke from Bangkok-based bartender Liam Baer. "First and foremost, this is not a drink for everyone," warns Baer. He kept scotch in the mix, but went for something more smoky than peaty and brought the artichoke-based Cynar center stage. "I wanted to highlight the often undetected vegetal notes in Cynar, so I added a little bit of saline to really make the artichoke shine," he explains. A quartet of orange peel zests—three incorporated into the mix, one used as garnish—bring a fresh lift of brightness to the whole affair.

Combine the scotch, Cynar, Brown Sugar Cordial, salt, and orange zests in a mixing glass filled with ice. Stir until chilled and strain into a double old-fashioned glass over a large ice cube. Garnish with the remaining orange zest.

BROWN SUGAR CORDIAL

MAKES 2½ CUPS

2 cups Demerara sugar

1 cup water

2 ounces Demerara rum

In a medium saucepan over medium heat, bring the Demerara sugar and water to a simmer, stirring the mixture occasionally to dissolve the sugar. At the first crack of a boil, remove from the heat. Once the syrup has cooled and thickened, stir in the rum, then store the cordial in a glass jar with a lid. The cordial will keep in the refrigerator for up to a month.

CRANBERRY BERET

MAKES I DRINK

1 orange wedge

12 fresh cranberries

1½ ounces Laird's Straight Apple Brandy

½ ounce Amaro CioCiaro

½ ounce Aperol

2 dashes cranberry bitters

Hard apple cider

Garnish: orange zest and 3 fresh cranberries, skewered

This is a reboot of a cocktail with a not-so-sexy name, Cranberry-Spice Cocktail, that I created for *Food and Wine* magazine. Cranberries, oranges, and apples are still at the heart of the drink, but I amped up the proof a bit with Laird's apple brandy and played off the bittersweet orange notes of the Amaro CioCiaro and brightness brought on by the Aperol. It's a great before-dinner drink to kick off a Thanksgiving gathering, a time when it's good to keep people busy with a drink in their hand. You can also batch it up as a punch and have your guests serve themselves.

Combine the orange wedge and cranberries in a cocktail shaker and muddle until the fruit is just broken up. Add the apple brandy, Amaro CioCiaro, Aperol, and bitters and fill with ice. Shake until chilled and double-strain into a collins glass filled with ice. Top off with the hard apple cider. Garnish with the orange zest and skewered cranberries.

CYNARA

I lived in Seattle for more than a decade and Tom Douglas's Palace Kitchen was where you could find me every Friday night. I make it a point to return to Seattle at least once a year, and immediately after dropping my bag off at the hotel, I head straight over to the Palace for a late-night Palace Burger Royale and immediately regret ever moving in the first place.

Former Palace Kitchen assistant manager Maggie Early created the Cynara and shared its origin story with me. "I had spent a few weeks on Lake Maggiore in Northern Italy with my family the fall before I was working at Palace Kitchen. We went there to spread my father's ashes on an island on the lake where he had visited a decade before and declared to my mom that he could die happy there." The rental house where they were staying had a fully stocked bar and that's where Maggie's love of Cynar started.

The centerpiece of the seemingly simple cocktail is a large, bitters-soaked ice cube that keeps the drink chilled while slowly rounding out the flavor as it melts. "When you first sip the cocktail, it's sweet, boozy, and pleasant, like all of its liquid components," Early explains. "As the ice cube starts to melt you get the rounded-out flavors from the bitters. It's the kind of drink you want to sip slowly and experience the change in flavor."

MAKES 1 DRINK

1½ ounces bourbon, preferably Buffalo Trace

½ ounce Cynar

½ ounce Aperol

Bitters ice cube (see Note)

Garnish: orange zest

....

Build the bourbon, Cynar, and Aperol in a double old-fashioned glass. Add the bitters ice cube. Garnish with the orange zest.

NOTE To make the bitters ice cube, use a silicone 2-inch ice cube tray filled with water and add 7 drops of Angostura bitters (or other aromatic bitters) into each cube before freezing.

EEYORE'S REQUIEM

MAKES I DRINK

1½ ounces
Campari

1 ounce Dolin
Blanc vermouth

½ ounce
Tanqueray gin

¼ ounce Cynar

¼ ounce
Fernet-Branca

2 dashes orange
bitters

Garnish: 3 orange
twists

Inspired by what he calls "the most bitter character in literature," Toby Maloney's Eeyore's Requiem is a "deep dark Negroni, turned on its head." The partner and head mixologist at the Violet Hour in Chicago and the Patterson House in Nashville starts with a base of bitter complexity by stacking three different amari amped up with aromatic French vermouth and juniper-rich gin. "This drink is an excellent foil to the sweet, bumbling, fruity drinks with very little brain," Maloney says.

....

Combine all the ingredients except the garnish in a mixing glass filled with ice. Stir until chilled and strain into a chilled coupe glass. Express the three orange twists over the surface of the drink, discarding the first two, and saving the third for garnish.

ELENA'S VIRTUE

MAKES I DRINK

1 ounce
Amaro Nonino
Quintessentia

½ ounce Amaro
Montenegro

½ ounce freshly
squeezed lime juice

¼ ounce Tuaca
liqueur

¼ ounce Luxardo
amaretto

Garnish: orange
zest and basil sprig

¼ ounce Amaro
Ramazzotti,
smoked (see Note)

"This was the last time that I ever really tried my hand at a cocktail competition," is how the story of the time my friend Andrew Bohrer entered a mai tai competition begins. "The mai tai is a ghost we project our ideas on—my mind was on amaro here. So I set out to make a mai tai that contains no rum, using only Italian liqueurs, many of which are bitter." The result was a complex yet inspiring drink that even prompted Jeffrey Morgenthaler to declare on his blog in 2011: "Now here was a drink with legs and a hint of what was to come in the world of cocktails, in my humble opinion."

....

Combine the Amaro Nonino, Amaro Montenegro, lime juice, Tuaca, and amaretto in a cocktail shaker filled with ice. Shake until chilled and strain into a Hurricane glass filled with crushed ice. Garnish with the orange zest and basil. Pour the smoked Amaro Ramazzotti amaro over the drink.

NOTE To smoke the Ramazzotti amaro, pour it into a decanter and use a handheld smoking gun to fill the decanter with smoke. While Bohrer may not wholeheartedly approve, you can also use regular nonsmoked Ramazzotti if you desire.

ELENA'S VIRTUE

EMBITTERED GARIBALDI

David Little's deconstructed take on the classic Garibaldi (page 94) is one of his favorite drinks at his amaro-centric Seattle bar, Barnacle. The bright orange sunset color of the Garibaldi takes a moody turn toward twilight with the addition of the dark and cooling Bràulio in this austere old-fashioned variation.

....

Combine the Amaro Bràulio, Amaro Montenegro, and salt in a mixing glass filled with ice. Stir until chilled and strain into a double old-fashioned glass over a large ice cube. Garnish with the lemon zest.

MAKES 1 DRINK

2 ounces Amaro Bràulio

1 ounce Amaro Montenegro

2 pinches of kosher salt

Garnish: lemon zest

EXIT STRATEGY

MAKES 1 DRINK

*1½ ounces
Amaro Nonino
Quintessentia*

*¾ ounce Germain-
Robin Craft-
Method Brandy*

*¼ ounce Amaro
Meletti*

Pinch of kosher salt

*Garnish: orange
twist*

With the Exit Strategy, Natasha David, co-owner and head bartender of the subterranean Lower East Side bar Nitecap, wanted to create a "rich and luscious, almost caramel-like old-fashioned using some of bartenders' favorite ingredients." As the proprietor of a popular late-night destination for her fellow bartenders, David should know a thing or two about what bartenders like to drink at the end of their shift. This cocktail hits on those prescriptive notes: "Not too boozy (don't want to be hungover the next day), comforting (they've been working hard all night), decadent (Amaro Nonino and brandy!)," she says.

Combine all the ingredients except the garnish in a mixing glass filled with ice. Stir until chilled and strain into a double old-fashioned glass over a large ice cube. Garnish with the orange twist.

FIELDS FOREVER

"Let me take you down, 'cause I'm going to Strawberry Fields."

MAKES I DRINK

1 fresh strawberry

1 ounce Foro
Amaro Speciale

¾ ounce Aperol

¼ ounce Campari

¾ ounce freshly
squeezed lemon
juice

½ ounce simple
syrup (page 118)

1 egg white

3 to 5 drops
Peychaud's Bitters

If it's on the menu when I'm drinking at the NoMad, chances are I'm ordering the summery Fields Forever. NoMad bar director Leo Robitschek points out that the drink is named after the Beatles' "Strawberry Fields Forever," and the song shares the name with a garden next to an orphanage where John Lennon used to play when he was a young boy. "The lyrics represent a beautiful and dark reprieve, much like this cocktail's easy-drinking but bitter nature," Robitschek says. It's a low-proof, bitter, and summery cocktail in a coupe glass and Robitschek, in particular, likes how the drink "showcases the citrus and mint tones of the Foro Amaro while complementing the strawberry flavors."

Cut the top off the strawberry, place the berry in a cocktail shaker, and muddle until lightly smashed. Add the Foro Amaro, Aperol, Campari, lemon juice, simple syrup, and egg white and dry shake (without ice) for at least 10 seconds to fully incorporate the egg white. Add ice and continue shaking until chilled and double-strain into a chilled coupe or cocktail glass. After the egg white foam settles, add drops of Peychaud's Bitters and gently twist the stem of the glass between your thumb and index finger to create a centrifugal force–enhanced design.

"Amaros are a very versatile ingredient and can be used as either a base or a modifier. I usually balance an amaro cocktail with egg white, cream, soda, or Champagne when I use it as a base. These ingredients help mellow the flavors in order to create a more balanced cocktail. I also like using them in sours as a split base with other higher-proof spirits, such as rye or gin."

—LEO ROBITSCHEK
The NoMad, New York, New York

FLIP YA FOR REAL

MAKES 1 DRINK

*1½ ounces
Fernet-Vallet*

*1 ounce Ancho
Reyes ancho chile
liqueur*

*½ ounce Demerara
syrup (see page 118)*

1 whole egg

*Garnish: freshly
grated cinnamon*

Before he makes his untimely exit in the 1995 film *The Usual Suspects*, Benicio del Toro's character Fred Fenster mumbles his way through the movie in an unintelligible yet wholly delightful manner. When talking back to detectives trying to interrogate him, Fenster utters his most memorable line from the film: "He'll flip ya. Flip ya for real." Inspired by this cinematic retort, I present a flip of my own, a spicy, bitter, and smoky-sweet affair (much like Fenster himself) that brings together two Mexican liqueurs. With notes of cinnamon and bitter flowers, Fernet-Vallet is softer than its Italian cousin Fernet-Branca, and the Ancho Reyes liqueur, based on a 1927 recipe from Puebla, Mexico, adds a smoky sweetness with just a bit of heat.

Combine all of the ingredients except the garnish in a cocktail shaker and dry shake (without ice) for at least 10 seconds to fully incorporate the egg. Add ice and continue shaking until chilled and double-strain into a chilled coupe or cocktail glass. Garnish with freshly grated cinnamon.

FOREGONE CONCLUSION

When it comes to demystifying amaro to customers new to his bar, Barnacle owner David Little likes to "meet people with an air of humility and empathy; I try to make this esoteric world accessible." His Foregone Conclusion is a dry and bitter take on the Boulevardier, with equal parts of rye and Gran Classico Bitter and a split base of Amaro Sibilla and Bäska Snaps rounding out the mix.

....

Combine all the ingredients except the garnish in a mixing glass filled with ice. Stir until chilled and strain into a chilled coupe or cocktail glass. Garnish with the orange zest.

MAKES 1 DRINK

1 ounce rye whiskey

1 ounce Gran Classico Bitter

½ ounce Amaro Sibilla

½ ounce Bäska Snaps med Malört

Garnish: orange zest

FRIÛL LIBAR

MAKES 1 DRINK

1½ ounces
Amaro Nonino
Quintessentia

½ ounce navy
strength gin,
preferably
Genius Navy

½ ounce freshly
squeezed lemon
juice

¼ ounce Demerara
syrup (see page 118)

2 dashes
Peychaud's Bitters

Garnish: lemon
zest

My friend Bill Mann used to be the general manager at Prime Meats in Brooklyn but now he's down in Austin, Texas, where he spent a few years holding the same position at Paul Qui's eponymous restaurant, Qui. When I stopped in to have dinner and catch up with him at Qui, he recommended I start with the Friûl Libar, a cocktail created by Justin Elliott, then the bar manager, that featured a local Texas gin and Amaro Nonino. When I asked about the name of the drink, Elliott told me *Friûl Libar*," or "free Friuli" is the slogan of the autonomy movement of the Friulian people in northeastern Italy, where Nonino is produced. While this cocktail doesn't share too much with the Cuba Libre, it is worth noting that there is some precedent for naming cocktails after the calls to arms graffitied by revolutionaries. But ultimately, he notes he has "at best, a cursory understanding of Friulian politics. Sometimes I just can't help but enjoy watching people wrestle with how to pronounce funny words." However you say it, the result is a winter-appropriate sour that is "light, drinkable, and most important, craveable."

Combine all of the ingredients except the garnish in a cocktail shaker filled with ice. Shake until chilled and double-strain into a chilled coupe or cocktail glass. Express the lemon peel over the surface of the drink, then, per Elliott, "garnish sexily" by putting a notch in the peel and affixing it to the glass. "I hate things floating around in my drink," he explains.

GATO AMARGO

I first met Tad Carducci while he was guest-bartending at Bellocq in New Orleans during Tales of the Cocktail. He was making a lineup of amaro-based cocktails, and if that wasn't enough to win me over, he was also a gracious and generous guy to talk with. Carducci, and his business partner, Paul Tanguay, comprise the well-traveled, high-volume bartending duo and industry consultants the Tippling Bros., and also the authors of the Mexican-inspired cocktail book, *The Tippling Bros: A Lime and a Shaker*.

In their book, you'll find the Gato Amargo ("bitter cat" in Spanish), a "playful and quaffable drink that's got some chutzpah," as Carducci puts it. This juicy, fruity long drink pairs Amaro Montenegro, one of the best examples of a gateway amaro, with bubbly orange soda rounded out with a kick of tequila. Carducci and Tanguay encourage you to seek out Mexican Fanta, which is made with pure cane sugar, instead of the syrupy sweet, high-fructose corn syrup that's used in the States. To give this bitter kitty a proper taste of la dolce vita, try it with a bottle of orange Fanta from Italy.

MAKES 1 DRINK

1 fresh strawberry, quartered

1 ounce blanco tequila

1 ounce Amaro Montenegro

½ ounce freshly squeezed lemon juice

3 ounces orange Fanta, preferably Mexican or Italian

Garnish: orange slice

Place the strawberry in a cocktail shaker and muddle until lightly smashed. Add the tequila, Amaro Montenegro, and lemon juice. Add ice and shake until chilled. Strain into a highball glass filled with crushed ice. Top off with the Fanta and stir to incorporate. Garnish with the orange slice.

GRANDMOTHER'S TEA

MAKES I DRINK

1 ounce Louis Royer Force 53 VSOP Cognac

1 ounce Dolin Blanc vermouth

½ ounce Vecchio Amaro del Capo

½ ounce Strega

1 dash Bittermens Orange Cream Citrate

Garnish: lemon twist and orange twist

"I had the good fortune of visiting Cognac and Jarnac in France with Nicolas Royer, the sixth generation of the venerable Louis Royer Cognac house," begins Sother Teague's tale of the origin of Grandmother's Tea. On that memorable trip, Teague, who runs New York's bitters bar Amor y Amargo, had the chance to visit Royer's *grand-mère* at her home on one of the vineyards. "Being a good Southern boy, I have a tremendous affection for my own grandmother, so I was excited by this notion. We arrived in the early afternoon and was greeted by his grandmother on the front porch of her beautiful home. She was as gracious as I expected and gave us a tour of the grounds and offered us pastry. It remains my fondest memory of the trip," he says. Back in New York, Teague went to work to create a cocktail in her honor, and recalling his own grandmother's fondness for iced tea, he looked to "mimic the flavors of Southern-style iced tea but pack the punch of 106-proof Cognac."

Combine all the ingredients except the garnish in a mixing glass filled with ice. Stir until chilled and strain into a rocks glass filled with ice. Express the oils from both the orange and lemon twists over the drink and neatly arrange in the glass.

"It's a good rule of thumb that the lighter-colored amari are generally better in warmer weather and darker, more viscous ones are warming and delicious in cooler months. But rules are made to be broken."

—SOTHER TEAGUE
Amor y Amargo, New York, New York

HERE TODAY, SAIGON AMARO

MAKES I DRINK

¾ ounce
Amaro Sibilla

¾ ounce Cynar

¾ ounce Carpano
Antiqua Formula
sweet vermouth

¾ ounce freshly
squeezed lime juice

½ ounce Saigon
Cinnamon Syrup
(recipe follows)

1 ounce soda water

Garnish: mint
sprig

This whimsically named drink was first featured on a particularly pun-driven cocktail menu at Nashville's Rolf and Daughters (that may have been the same menu where I once ordered a Cynar-nold Palmer). "I wanted to create a light, bitter, amaro-driven cocktail that could be drunk as easily at the beginning of the meal or the end of one," says bar director Brice Hoffman. "The Amaro Sibilla brings a heavier alcohol presence as well as an intense bitterness mixed with honey and nutty elements." The sweeter Cynar and Carpano Antiqua sweet vermouth continue the play of bitter and sweet ingredients, "creating something challenging for the palate but also approachable." The Saigon Cinnamon Syrup plays well with the herbal notes of the three primary spirits, and the bright acidity from the lime juice and crisp soda water "help to lighten up what would otherwise be a quite heavy drink," notes Hoffman.

Combine the Amaro Sibilla, Cynar, sweet vermouth, lime juice, and cinnamon syrup in a cocktail shaker filled with ice. Shake until chilled and double-strain into a collins glass filled with ice. Top with soda water. Garnish with a lightly spanked mint sprig.

SAIGON CINNAMON SYRUP

MAKES
APPROXIMATELY
1½ CUPS

½ tablespoon
ground Saigon
cinnamon powder

1 cup water

1 cup sugar

In a medium saucepan over medium heat, mix the Saigon cinnamon into the water, then add the sugar. At the first crack of a boil, remove from the heat. Allow to cool for 15 minutes, then strain through damp cheesecloth into a glass jar with a lid. The syrup will keep in the refrigerator up to a month.

HUNTING VEST

"On the West Coast, amaro has been a big part of drinking culture since Fernet-Branca blew up in San Francisco," says Portland's Evan Zimmerman. Playing around with spirited infusions like cherry liqueur and Lapsang souchong tea or Cynar and Stumptown coffee beans has long been a favorite pastime of Zimmerman, who heads up North+Lands, a boutique cocktail consulting group. When he helped open the Woodsman Tavern, the Hunting Vest, his decidedly Pacific Northwest take on the classic Old Pal cocktail, quickly became the most popular drink on the menu. The Cedar-Infused Campari used in the cocktail brings a bit of the woodsy outdoors into your coupe glass, but is delicious sipped on its own or chilled over ice.

MAKES 1 DRINK

1 ounce Cedar-Infused Campari (recipe follows)

1 ounce dry vermouth

½ ounce rye whiskey

½ ounce fino sherry

Lemon zest

Combine the Cedar-Infused Campari, vermouth, rye, and sherry in a mixing glass filled with ice. Stir until chilled and strain into a chilled coupe or cocktail glass. Express the lemon zest over the surface of the glass and discard.

CEDAR-INFUSED CAMPARI

Break up the cedar planks into pieces small enough to fit into a quart-sized Mason jar. The number of cedar planks needed will vary depending on their size, but you want enough to fill up the jar (approximately 3 cups of chips). Place the cedar on a fireproof surface, like a metal baking sheet. Using a kitchen torch, burn the pieces of cedar until well charred.

MAKES 3 TO 4 CUPS

1 to 3 untreated food-safe cedar planks, broken into small pieces

3 to 4 cups Campari

Once cooled, place the cedar in a 1-quart Mason jar with a lid. Cover the cedar chunks with Campari. Allow to sit, undisturbed and out of direct sunlight, for 2 weeks.

Strain the Campari, discarding the chunks of cedar. Strain again three times, using damp cheesecloth. Store in a glass container or bottle with a lid. The infused Campari will keep for up to a year and can be enjoyed on its own chilled over ice.

ICE-BERG

MAKES 1 DRINK

1 ounce Pueblo Viejo reposado tequila

1 bottle Underberg

1 ounce orgeat, preferably Orgeat Works T'Orgeat toasted almond syrup

¾ ounce freshly squeezed lemon juice

If you're talking to Brooklyn bartender Garret Richard, then the topic of tiki drinks will likely—scratch that, definitely—come up. You can now find him wearing his custom-made bolo ties behind the stick at New York's Happiest Hour and their sister bar Slowly Shirley, but when he was working at Prime Meats under the tutelage of Damon Boelte, he developed a great appreciation for the German digestif Underberg. "My style is, and will always have, a tropical bent, so incorporating a heavy bitter into a tiki drink seemed like a hard task," he says. "But with its strong clove and spice notes, Underberg provides a wonderful canvas to demonstrate some exotic flair."

His eureka moment came on a hot summer day when bartender Thomas Waugh was day drinking at one of the sidewalk tables outside the bar. "He drank margaritas with an Underberg shot on the side throughout the afternoon. Channeling the Cabo-style Mexican Bulldog, I decided to make a frozen margarita with an Underberg bottle in it just to be playful." After that, it became an off-the-menu hit among the regulars. Mixing Underberg into a cocktail had been done before, but making the tiny bottle part of the actual garnish—something that's catching on among bartenders—was first documented on that illustrated place mat menu at Prime Meats' Tiki Takeover.

Combine the tequila, Underberg (reserving the bottle), orgeat, and lemon juice in a blender. Blend with 1 cup crushed ice until fluffy. Pour into a chilled coupe or cocktail glass. Garnish with the empty bottle of Underberg.

ITALIAN BUCK

MAKES 1 DRINK

1½ ounces Cynar

1½ ounces Amaro Montenegro

¾ ounce freshly squeezed lime juice

3 ounces ginger beer

Garnish: lime wheel

The implied kick in the category of drinks known as the Buck comes from the addition of spicy ginger ale or ginger beer. Most bucks have a bourbon base, but Jamie Boudreau's Italian Buck lives up to its name with a split base of Cynar and Amaro Montenegro, resulting in a refreshing and bittersweet long drink.

Boudreau's Seattle bar, Canon Whiskey and Bitters Emporium, continues to garner global accolades, including a Tales of the Cocktail Spirited Award for World's Best Spirits Selection, and in his book *The Canon Cocktail Book*, he shares his philosophy of running a successful bar, along with dozens of his signature recipes. He also has a deep selection of amari, and just in case you've got an extra grand to burn, you can have a taste of vintage Amer Picon from 1890 for $950.

....

Combine all the ingredients except the garnish in a cocktail shaker filled with ice. Shake until chilled and strain into a chilled collins glass. Garnish with the lime wheel.

THE JUMP OFF

I first met Raleigh chef Ashley Christensen at the Southern Foodways Symposium in Oxford, Mississippi, and if I remember it correctly, there was a flask of bourbon involved. She is among the kindest (and coolest) people I know and her generosity knows no bounds. After my book *Bitters* came out, she invited me down to Raleigh and hosted me at Fox Liquor Bar for a bitters talk and tasting with the local bartending community (she also made sure I never went hungry and sent me back to my hotel each night with a to-go container of chess pie).

This Fox Liquor Bar original is a joint creation from bar manager John Parra and head bartender Garrett Waddell. The name the Jump Off is lifted from a Plastic Little song, and according to Parra, it's the placeholder title the Fox crew uses for any cocktail in the early stages of development. This "tiki in a coupe," as Parra calls it, weaves in the fruity character of Amaro Montenegro "in a fun, unconventional, yet nevertheless relatable fashion." Parra stresses, "It's important that the Jump Off achieves this accessibility without hiding the character of the Montenegro, but by highlighting appealing aspects of it."

MAKES 1 DRINK

¾ ounce Amaro Montenegro

¾ ounce Bols genever

½ ounce Cointreau

¾ ounce freshly squeezed lemon juice

¼ ounce passion fruit puree

Grapefruit zest

Combine all the ingredients except the grapefruit zest in a cocktail shaker filled with ice. Shake until chilled and double-strain into a chilled coupe or cocktail glass. Express the grapefruit zest over the surface of the drink and discard.

"We really don't like to overcomplicate things when we serve amari in our bar. They are deep and complex, and enormous enjoyment can be had just by sipping them simply, with a bit of chill on ice and opened up with proper dilution. On the rock with a swath of citrus and a splash of club soda is likewise delightful. In the context of a cocktail, we work toward the goal of thoughtfully enhancing their tremendous character in interesting, but respectful, ways."

—JOHN PARRA
Fox Liquor Bar, Raleigh, North Carolina

JUNIPER #3

MAKES 1 DRINK

*1 ounce
barrel-aged gin*

*¾ ounce Rothman
and Winter
Orchard Apricot
Liqueur*

½ ounce Campari

*¾ ounce freshly
squeezed lemon
juice*

Pinch of kosher salt

"This drink came about as a way for us to feature barrel-aged gin," says John deBary, bar director for the Momofuku restaurant group, of the Juniper #3, a drink featured at Momofuku Ssäm Bar. "It tasted like someone was making a whiskey sour and a Negroni at the same time and accidentally poured them into the same glass."

Combine all the ingredients in a cocktail shaker filled with a large ice cube. Shake until chilled and strain into a chilled double old-fashioned glass.

LETTERS OF MARQUE

MAKES 1 DRINK

*1 ounce Scarlet Ibis
rum*

1 ounce Cynar

*½ ounce Pierre
Ferrand dry
curaçao*

½ ounce Galliano

*Garnish: flamed
orange zest
(page 118)*

I'll forever hold a spot on my mantel for any drink from Jerry Slater, the owner of H. Harper Station in Atlanta. My first public book signing for *Bitters* was at the Southern Foodways Symposium in Oxford, Mississippi, at a reception where visiting authors were spread out around the room standing next to a small stack of their book. David Wondrich and I were the lone drinks writers among the well-seasoned cookbook authors, and as we took our places, he said with a smirk, "Welcome to the cocktail book ghetto, where drinks books sell one copy for every ten cookbooks." And then, almost on cue, Slater came over to introduce himself and buy a book, and he instantly became the very first person with a signed copy of my book. Whenever I see him in Oxford each fall, I still remember to thank him.

The name Letters of Marque refers to the government documents that authorized privateers to profit from possessions seized at sea. "A license to pirate, basically," offers Slater. "I really prefer Scarlet Ibis rum from Trinidad in this cocktail; it has a beautiful richness that balances the unique vegetal bitterness of the Cynar perfectly."

Combine all the ingredients except the garnish in a mixing glass filled with ice. Stir until chilled and strain into a chilled coupe or cocktail glass. Garnish with the flamed orange zest.

JUNIPER #3

LITTLE ITALY

This 2005 cocktail from New York cocktail icon Audrey Saunders is true to its name, with a combination of classic Italian and American ingredients: spicy American rye mixed with the vegetal, bittersweet Cynar and sweet, herbal Italian vermouth. This variation on the classic Manhattan has become the constant drink I order when I'm looking for something brown, bitter, and stirred at the end of the night. A little splash of cherry syrup in the mixing glass would also be welcome.

MAKES 1 DRINK

2 ounces rye whiskey

½ ounce Cynar

¾ ounce sweet vermouth

Garnish: 3 cocktail cherries, skewered

Combine the rye, Cynar, and sweet vermouth in a mixing glass filled with ice. Stir until chilled and strain into a chilled coupe or cocktail glass. Garnish with the skewered cherries.

M&M

After strolling through the picturesque alleyways and bridges of Ascoli Piceno with brothers Matteo and Mauro Meletti, we joined the rest of their family for aperitivi at Caffè Meletti in Piazza del Popolo, in the heart of the city center. This historic Art Nouveau building originally served as the Royal Post Office but was purchased by Matteo and Mauro's great-great-grandfather in 1903 and turned into a café patronized by the likes of Hemingway and Sartre.

The Melettis no longer own the café, but when your name is emblazoned across a building, you can be sure that you're welcomed with open arms when you walk through the door. We gathered around a corner banquette with Matteo and Mauro and their parents Silvio and Louisa and their uncle Aldo. Marco Pompili, the silver-haired barman, who, despite the heat wave, remained cool in a white jacket and black necktie, rolled a bar cart to our tables and, executing each simple gesture with a dignified flourish, crafted three cocktails using the café's namesake spirits.

The first drink was made with equal parts Amaro Meletti and their 1870 Bitter, a ruby-colored aperitivo-style bitter they had recently released, and united with four hearty dashes of Angostura bitters. As we raised our glasses, Matteo explained that the drink was invented by his mother, Louisa, who nodded in approval after we clinked glasses. When I asked what it was called, Matteo said, "It has no name. Maybe you'll call it something you like?" Now, whenever I have this drink I think back to that hot summer night with the Melettis. I've taken to calling it the M&M, honoring the initials of the two Meletti bittersweet liqueurs used to make it and for my hosts, Matteo and Mauro.

....

Combine the Amaro Meletti, 1870 Bitter, and bitters in a mixing glass filled with ice. Stir until chilled and strain into an old-fashioned glass over crushed ice. Garnish with the orange slice.

MAKES 1 DRINK

1 ounce Amaro Meletti

1 ounce Meletti 1870 Bitter

4 dashes Angostura bitters

Garnish: orange slice

THE MAYOR'S LAMENT

MAKES 1 DRINK

1½ ounces rye whiskey, preferably Rittenhouse

1 ounce Amaro Nardini

3 dashes Woodford Reserve Spiced Cherry Bitters

3 dashes Regans' Orange Bitters No. 6

2 dashes Peychaud's Bitters

A few years back a mutual friend introduced me to Nashville chef Matt Bolus, and we shared some e-mails on the subject of bitters as he was preparing to open his restaurant, the 404 Kitchen. On my first visit to Nashville I had the chance to finally meet Matt in person over dinner at the bar of his restaurant, which is connected to the 404 Hotel in a converted shipping container.

That night at the 404 Kitchen, the first cocktail I tried was the Mayor's Lament, created by Travis Brazil, 404's general manager and sommelier. The drink was created and named for 404 Kitchen regular Eric Close, who played Mayor Teddy Conrad on the TV series *Nashville*. Brazil told me, "He is a big fan of American whiskey and I love a good amaro, so I thought this would be a great way to introduce the distinctive minty, herbal notes of the Nardini amaro to him." He then amped up the bitters as a key ingredient to bridge the drink, deciding on using three different kinds—orange, cherry, and Peychaud's—to "highlight their own properties while complementing the others." Close's character had just taken a drastic arc toward the dark side on the series and Brazil thought "the cocktail named after him would be a great opportunity for a 'character study of bitters.'"

Combine all the ingredients in a mixing glass filled with ice. Stir until chilled and strain into a double old-fashioned glass over a large ice cube.

MONTE CLIFT

"Nobody ever lies about being lonely."

—MONTGOMERY CLIFT AS ROBERT E. LEE "PREW" PREWITT
From Here to Eternity

I was a bit of a theater geek in high school, and when I went off to college, I had aspirations of treading the boards on the campus stage. I ended up as a double major in English and theater and was cast in several plays, but after my sophomore year, I switched gears to pursue writing. During my theater days, I was pretty obsessed with James Dean and Montgomery Clift and read every book I could find about them. Even though I was being cast as "Drunk Santa" in a stage adaptation of a musical version of *Miracle on 34th Street*, in my head, I was a moody, Method-acting misfit in a rumpled tweed jacket and tortoiseshell glasses. I used to keep a dog-eared mass-market paperback edition of Patricia Bosworth's 1978 biography of Clift tucked into my coat pocket to read between classes.

This bittersweet tribute to Monty features Mister Katz's Rock and Rye from Brooklyn's New York Distilling Company. On its own it's like a cocktail in a glass, with rye flavored with cinnamon, citrus, sour cherries, and rock candy sugar, and the Amaro Montenegro punches up the sweetness with a burst of orange and tangerine and a mild hint of herbal bitterness. Let's imagine him mixing up a pitcher of these for Elizabeth Taylor.

MAKES I DRINK

1½ ounces New York Distilling Company Mister Katz's Rock and Rye

1 ounce Amaro Montenegro

¼ ounce freshly squeezed lemon juice

2 dashes Hella Bitter citrus bitters

Garnish: orange zest and cocktail cherry

Combine all the ingredients except the garnish in a cocktail shaker filled with ice. Shake until chilled and strain into a double old-fashioned glass over a large ice cube. Garnish with the orange zest and cocktail cherry.

MUSTACHE RIDE

MAKES 1 DRINK

1½ ounces bourbon, preferably Bulleit

½ ounce Cynar

¾ ounce freshly squeezed lemon juice

½ ounce Joey Sunshine's Maple Simple Syrup (page 178)

½ ounce St. Elizabeth Allspice Dram

Garnish: lemon twist and cocktail cherry

Anna Wallace and Joe Sundberg are just two of the many distinguished alumni from chef Renee Erickson's the Walrus and the Carpenter who have gone on to enrich the Seattle food scene with their own contributions. Anna now owns the Seattle Seltzer Company and Joe is a partner at the restaurant Manolin. The Mustache Ride was a drink they collaborated on during the early days of W and C, sparked when the guys on staff started a high-stakes mustache-growing competition. Even customers got in on the action, donning elaborate fake mustaches and laying down odds on staff favorites likely to win. Wallace recalls, "At one point, we even caught a group of women rating the mustaches on the back of their oyster list." Wallace and Sundberg decided to feed the frenzy with a drink to commemorate the event, and the Mustache Ride was born.

"The drink is very similar to a Lion's Tail, though the replacement of simple syrup with a warming, but not too sweet Grade B maple syrup blows the true classic out of the water," states Wallace. She was making her own allspice dram but switched to St. Elizabeth Allspice Dram when she couldn't keep up with the demand. "Bulleit stands up to the complex flavors, but Cynar was really the dark horse in this race," she continues. "It adds a wonderful mouthfeel that truly completes the cocktail. It ramps the bitterness up to balance out the sweetness." Ladies and gentlemen, we have a winner.

Combine all of the ingredients except the garnish in a cocktail shaker filled with ice. Shake until chilled and strain into a chilled double old-fashioned glass. Garnish with the lemon twist and cocktail cherry.

"If I turn to an amaro in a cocktail, it's typically because I want to fatten the drink up while simultaneously adding that deep layer of bitterness that you'd get from a nonpotable bitter. The key to a successful cocktail with amaro is balance."

—ANNA WALLACE
Seattle Seltzer Company, Seattle, Washington

JOEY SUNSHINE'S MAPLE SIMPLE SYRUP

**MAKES
APPROXIMATELY
2½ CUPS**

*2 cups Grade B
maple syrup*

1 cup filtered water

*½ tablespoon black
peppercorns*

*½ tablespoon
fennel seeds*

*½ tablespoon
cloves*

*½ tablespoon
allspice berries*

*½ teaspoon freshly
grated nutmeg*

1 star anise pod

1 fresh bay leaf

In a medium saucepan over medium heat, combine all the ingredients. Bring to a simmer, stirring occasionally. At the first crack of a boil, remove from the heat. Let cool completely, then strain the syrup and discard the solids. Store the syrup in a glass jar with a lid. The syrup will keep refrigerated for up to a month.

PAPER PLANE

PAPER PLANE

I bet most of you can't think of the Paper Plane without automatically hearing the "All I wanna do is . . ." refrain from the M.I.A. song "Paper Planes." Sam Ross, a partner at New York's Attaboy, admits he was "playing the hell out of it" when he created this modern classic in 2008. Ross's equal-parts riff on the classic Last Word started with Amaro Nonino, "my absolute favorite amaro of all time." The first printed version of the Paper Plane had Campari, but Ross swapped in Aperol for better balance. Rye, scotch, applejack, and rum were up for the final component, but, Ross says, "bourbon remained the perfect complement" to the cocktail.

MAKES 1 DRINK

¾ *ounce bourbon*

¾ *ounce Aperol*

¾ *ounce Amaro Nonino Quintessentia*

¾ *ounce freshly squeezed lemon juice*

Combine all the ingredients in a cocktail shaker filled with ice. Shake until chilled and strain into a chilled coupe or cocktail glass.

RED HOOK CRITERIUM

MAKES I DRINK

1½ ounces Zucca Rabarbaro Amaro

½ ounce gin

1½ ounces freshly squeezed grapefruit juice

½ ounce freshly squeezed lemon juice

½ ounce simple syrup (page 118)

Soda water

Garnish: grapefruit twist

Every March since the late 2000s, a bike race called the Red Hook Criterium (known as "the Crit") tears through the Brooklyn waterfront neighborhood it's named after. St. John Frizell has held a box seat to this spectacle from his perch at his bar Fort Defiance on Van Brunt Street. He recalls the early days of the race as an "unsanctioned, unsponsored, ad hoc race conducted without official permission in the middle of the night on Red Hook's cobblestone streets," with a vivid memory of witnessing three stacked tiers of bikes locked to the chain link at the 2010 after-party held at a third-floor walk-up across from the bar.

The race got bigger, and with that came sponsorship and additional races around the world in Barcelona, London, and Milan. Frizell commemorated the first Milan race with a special cocktail. "After all, this was the biggest sporting event to happen in Red Hook since Sir Thomas Lipton docked the *Shamrock II* during the America's Cup in Erie Basin back in 1899," he says. He reached for the Zucca Rabarbaro, the Milanese amaro that had just become available in the United States, and put it "front and center" in a lighter drink, so that "you could conceivably ride a bike after having one or two." This "bitter and juicy highball" has remained on the menu ever since and is one of the greatest hits at Fort Defiance, especially during Crit Week.

Combine all the ingredients except the soda water and the garnish in a cocktail shaker filled with ice. Shake until chilled and strain into a highball glass filled with ice. Top off with soda water. Garnish with the grapefruit twist.

RICKEY RAMAZZOTTI

A Ramazzotti rickey is one thing, but Rickey Ramazzotti sounds like a decent guy from the neighborhood. He's the guy you call to help you move out of your apartment. This is my bitter take on the cherry limeade from Sonic Drive-In, which, when you're on foot and not behind the wheel, is even better when spiked with bourbon. I've always loved the root-beer spice notes of Ramazzotti—especially how they work together with the orange and vanilla from the bourbon and the brightness of the lime.

....

Place the cherries, lime wedges, and simple syrup in a cocktail shaker and muddle until the fruit is just broken up. Add the bourbon and Amaro Ramazzotti and fill with ice. Shake until chilled and double-strain into a double old-fashioned glass filled with ice (if you have pebble ice, even better). Top off with soda water. Garnish with the lime wedge and 2 cherries.

MAKES 1 DRINK

6 cherries, pitted

2 lime wedges

½ ounce simple syrup (page 118)

1 ounce bourbon

1 ounce Amaro Ramazzotti

Soda water

Garnish: lime wedge and 2 cherries

ROOT DOWN

MAKES I DRINK

1¼ ounces Cocchi Vermouth di Torino

¾ ounce El Dorado 12-year Demerara rum

½ ounce Art in the Age Root Liqueur

5 drops Bittermens Xocolatl Mole Bitters

5 drops Laphroaig 10-year Islay single-malt scotch

It's just one letter that separates *Parson* from *Parsons*, but upon my first visit to my almost-namesake restaurant, I instantly felt a surname-inspired kinship with the Chicago restaurant Parson's Chicken and Fish. Hot chicken, fried fish, hush puppies, and serious cocktails are all part of the program in this fun and funky Logan Square outpost. You can find the recipe for bar manager Charlie Schott's signature Negroni Slushy in Gary Regan's wonderful book, *The Negroni*, so rather than offering a cover version of that already perfect drink, I asked Schott for another favorite amaro drink from the menu to share. The Root Down inverts the classic spirit/vermouth ratio, with a healthy pour of Cocchi Vermouth di Torino. Based on a recipe from 1891, the Moscato-based vermouth comes together with the barky, herbal notes of Philadelphia's Art in the Age Root Liqueur. Mole bitters and a float of smoky single-malt scotch bring a well-balanced finish to this bittersweet sipper.

....

Combine the vermouth, rum, Root Liqueur, and bitters in a mixing glass filled with ice. Stir until chilled and strain into a chilled coupe or cocktail glass. Float the Laphroaig scotch on top.

SAFE PASSAGE

In the Ballard neighborhood of Seattle, Brandon Pettit had long been experimenting with his own small-batch shrubs, bitters, ginger beer, and liqueurs at Delancey—the popular pizzeria he runs with his wife, writer Molly Wizenberg—but when the vintage umbrella shop next door closed up, the couple turned it into a twelve-stool craft cocktail bar called Essex. You'll find sparkling Americano cocktails on tap and many of the drinks are doctored with house-made amaro and liqueurs. Spiked with Castelvetrano olive brine, the Safe Passage was created by Delancey's then bar manager Kenaniah Bystrom as a tribute to Brooklyn restaurant Franny's Sweet Olive cocktail for a party they hosted in honor of the Franny's cookbook release. The resulting drink is the perfect balance of salty, sweet, and bitter.

....

Combine the Nardini, Aperol, lemon juice, and olive brine in a cocktail shaker filled with ice. Shake until chilled and strain into a chilled coupe or cocktail glass. Top with Prosecco and garnish with the Castelvetrano olives.

MAKES 1 DRINK

1 ounce Amaro Nardini

¼ ounce Aperol

¼ ounce freshly squeezed lemon juice

¼ ounce olive brine from Castelvetrano olives

2½ ounces Prosecco or other sparkling wine

*Garnish:
2 Castelvetrano olives, skewered*

SAN FRANCISCO TREAT

1 ounce Fernet-Branca

1 ounce Averna

1 ounce Dolin Blanc vermouth

Garnish: flamed orange zest (page 118)

Bar manager Sam Levy is one of the first people you see upon entering the three Michelin–starred Restaurant at Meadowood in Saint Helena, California, and you'd be remiss if you didn't begin your soon-to-be unforgettable dining experience without first taking a seat at the bar to sample one of his creations. He'll also be happy to see you for an after-dinner drink, where he might serve you his signature San Francisco Treat. Named for the catchy Rice-A-Roni jingle, this equal-parts sipper unites Fernet-Branca, Averna, and Dolin Blanc vermouth. Levy says, "I wanted to soften the Fernet up with other things I love to use in cocktails. The Averna rounds it out and the Dolin Blanc softens everything, adding a delicate floral side. As a bartender, one thing I think I know is that most San Franciscans love Fernet. Adding the Averna and Dolin Blanc turned it into a treat."

Combine the Fernet-Branca, Averna, and vermouth in a mixing glass filled with ice. Stir until chilled and strain into a chilled double old-fashioned glass. Garnish with the flamed orange zest.

"When working on new cocktails, I usually try and substitute a standard ingredient like simple syrup, triple sec, or some such liquor for an amaro. My go-tos are always Amaro Nonino and Averna. Using amari for me is always about depth and roundness. I want the cocktail to be spirituous, sweet, sour, bitter, fruity, and floral, but the most important thing is balance. Tasting all ingredients together and separately is the key to a cocktail that will go on the list. My secret is using amaro to add depth and richness to an otherwise light or simplistic cocktail—instead of adding sugar, add amaro."

—SAM LEVY
The Restaurant at Meadowood, Saint Helena, California

SENEGALESE FRIENDSHIP BRACELET

"Cause everybody hates a tourist / Especially one who thinks it's all just a laugh."

No matter how savvy a traveler you think you might be, there are those unexpected moments when it feels like you've got a great big SUCKER bull's-eye stamped on your forehead. I was in Milan with photographer Ed Anderson and we had just followed in the footsteps of Verdi and Toscanini, enjoying a civilized aperitivo of an Americano and a Garibaldi while standing at the marble bar at Caffè Camparino in the Galleria Vittorio Emanuele II.

We stepped outside the bar, and wanting to avoid the crowds, leaned against the wall and pulled out our phones to look up the address for our next destination. In an instant, a buoyant man decked out in colorful robes whisked between us and greeted us with a hearty "America!" He told us he was from Senegal and that he loved the United States. When he asked where we lived, he smiled and shouted back, "Brooklyn! California!" and more curiously, "Michael Jackson! Michael Jordan!" In the midst of all of this jolly banter, he had not so subtly wrapped a rainbow-colored friendship bracelet snugly around each of our wrists. He insisted they were free but his open palm seemed to imply that wasn't the case. We may have lost two Euros, but we gained matching souvenirs for the remainder of our trip through Italy. In a nod to the Americano, I've paired two herbaceous spirits to represent my journey from Brooklyn to Milan: Campari from Milan and the tart, floral, and hibiscus-based Sorel liqueur made in Red Hook, a stone's throw from my apartment. Here's to you, my Senegalese friend!

MAKES 1 DRINK

1½ ounces Campari

1 ounce Sorel liqueur

Soda water

Garnish: lemon zest and orange zest

Build the Campari and Sorel liqueur in a highball glass filled with ice. Top off with soda water. Stir and garnish with the lemon and orange zests. You can get really fancy and braid the two garnishes together.

SEVENTH HEAVEN

MAKES 1 DRINK

1½ ounces Banks 7 Golden Age rum

½ ounce Neisson Blanc agricole rhum

½ ounce Amaro di Angostura

½ ounce freshly squeezed lime juice

¼ ounce Pistachio Orgeat (recipe follows)

¼ ounce Giffard crème de cacao blanc

1 barspoon Vieux Pontarlier absinthe

Garnish: mint sprig, lime wheel, and grated pistachio

This bittersweet tiki drink from bartender Adam Schmidt made its debut on the winter 2015 menu at PDT. Schmidt calls it a "a Zombie–mai tai mash-up and an ode to old-school tiki," pointing out his homage to tiki legend Donn Beach's "classic combination of Angostura and absinthe."

Combine all the ingredients except the absinthe and garnish in a cocktail shaker filled with ice. Shake until chilled and strain into a chilled tiki mug filled with pebble ice. Garnish with the mint sprig, lime wheel, and grated pistachio, then top with the absinthe.

PISTACHIO ORGEAT

MAKES 2¾ CUPS

1 (11-ounce) can Love'n Bake pistachio nut paste

11 ounces simple syrup (page 118)

Combine the pistachio paste and simple syrup in a bowl and mix with an immersion blender until smooth. Alternatively, add the ingredients to a blender and mix until smooth. The orgeat will keep in the refrigerator for up to 2 weeks.

SHARPIE MUSTACHE

One of the most recognized (at least most Instagrammed) and well-traveled drinks to come out of New York's Amor y Amargo is the Sharpie Mustache. That it's served in a small glass flask adorned with a mustache sticker certainly helps elevate it beyond the standard coupe glass experience, and it doesn't hurt that it's delicious, complex, well balanced, and pleasantly boozy.

Chris Elford now lives in Seattle, but when he was at Amor y Amargo in 2011 and 2012, he spent months tasting and playing around with the bar's dozens of bottles of amari on the shelf. He happened to be on a Meletti kick when "an older woman with a gruff voice who seemed like she was no stranger to drinking" came into the bar and ordered "whatever you like to make." Splitting the bases, rye and gin seemed like "strange but awesome bedfellows," and the tiki bitters and orange twist "made the drink pop just right."

And about that name? "I named it the Sharpie Mustache because, well, this drink is very, very boozy—deceptively so—and one of my favorite frat boy inclinations in America is that of drawing a Sharpie mustache on some poor soul who passed out early. I believe the rule is they are fair game if they still have their shoes on."

MAKES 1 DRINK

¾ ounce dry gin, preferably Rutte

¾ ounce rye whiskey, preferably Rittenhouse

¾ ounce Amaro Meletti

¾ ounce Bonal Gentiane-Quina

1 dash Bittermens 'Elemakule Tiki bitters

Garnish: orange zest

Combine all the ingredients except the garnish in a mixing glass filled with ice. Stir until chilled and strain into a chilled old-fashioned glass. Express the orange zest over the surface of the drink and use as a garnish.

"My biggest amaro tip is not to force it and not to overthink it. Blind tasting is the way to go if you truly want to know what your own unbiased opinions on these products are, and don't be afraid to use a tempered hand when adding them to cocktails."

—CHRIS ELFORD
Rob Roy, Seattle, Washington

SKYSTONE MELETTI

MAKES I DRINK

2 ounces Glenlivet 12 year single-malt scotch

1 ounce Amaro Meletti

½ ounce orgeat

2 dashes orange bitters

Spuma Paoletti or ginger ale

Garnish: orange zest

On my last night in Ascoli Piceno, a small town in central Italy, after an evening of cocktails, wine, and dinner with the Meletti family, we walked across Piazza del Popolo in the shadows of the historic buildings and stopped into the small but lively Bar Sestili for one last drink.

Owner and bartender Fabio Caponi welcomed us and immediately went to work behind the bar, where he created a special drink in our honor. With two generations of the town's storied Meletti family sitting at the tables outside, Fabio naturally reached for a bottle of Amaro Meletti, which he said matched perfectly with a vintage bottle of 12-year-old Glenlivet. "A gift from my beloved grandfather. I like to think this cocktail celebrates his memory, too."

When I checked back in with him to get the recipe, he shared this advice on the drink: "Skystone Meletti is my tribute to the Meletti family and to Ascoli Piceno. I suggest enjoying it as a meditative drink under the stars—in a cozy corner, ideally within Ascoli's marble buildings, with great company, as it was originally created and first tasted." I'm looking forward to returning back there someday soon for more drinks under the stars.

....

Combine the scotch, Amaro Meletti, orgeat, and bitters in cocktail shaker filled with ice. Shake until chilled and strain into a highball glass filled with ice. Top off with the Spuma Paoletti or ginger ale. Garnish with orange zest.

SMITHSTREETER

I am proud to be a member of the so-called mug club at Prime Meats in Carroll Gardens, Brooklyn. For a onetime fee, you become the proud owner of your own mug, which is kept behind the bar just awaiting your arrival. I was happy with my status as mug number 24 (doesn't that make me one of the top twenty-five regulars?)—until I met Chris DeCrosta, owner of mug 1. DeCrosta lives a few blocks away from the bar, and whenever I see him, he's usually at his favorite stool (B1). But before I actually met him, I only knew him by his Instagram handle, @smithstreeter. He's inked up and obsessed with the brand Supreme and casts a cool, laid-back vibe, typically decked out in a T-shirt and ball cap. For the longest time, I thought he might be a fourth Beastie Boy, but it turns out he's a successful retail real estate specialist. I always love running into him and wanted to create a drink in tribute to our friendship—something that I could envision him drinking from his favorite stool. Stay bitter, Chris!

MAKES 1 DRINK

1 ounce rye whiskey

¾ ounce Amaro Lucano

½ ounce cold-brew coffee

¼ ounce Demerara syrup (see page 118)

2 dashes orange bitters

Tonic water

Garnish: lemon zest

Combine the rye, Amaro Lucano, cold-brew coffee, Demerara syrup, and orange bitters in a mixing glass filled with ice. Stir until chilled and strain into a highball glass filled with crushed ice. Top off with tonic water. Add more crushed ice if needed. Garnish with the lemon zest.

SUMMER BABE (WINTER VERSION)

MAKES I DRINK

1½ ounces Mount Gay Black Barrel rum

1 ounce Amaro Ramazzotti

6 fresh blackberries

½ ounce freshly squeezed lime juice

¼ ounce Demerara syrup (see page 118)

Ginger beer

Garnish: lime wedge and 2 fresh blackberries

"But she waits there in the levee wash, mixing cocktails with a plastic-tipped cigar."

You didn't think you'd get through this bittersweet cocktail playlist of mine without coming across a drink named after a Pavement song, did you? Granted, fresh blackberries aren't exactly in season in the colder months, but I envisioned a drink that would be appropriate as a cool refresher in the humid days of August and as a spicy cooler for the change of seasons. For the summer version, you can pack your glass with ice, and in winter, fill your glass with one large ice cube for ease of dilution (and seasonal contemplation). The blackberries bring a kick to the fruity notes and toasted char finish of the rum and bitter orange from the Ramazzotti, along with a bright and spicy kick from the lime and ginger beer. Plastic-tipped cigar garnish optional.

Combine the rum, Amaro Ramazzotti, blackberries, lime juice, and Demerara syrup in a cocktail shaker filled with ice. Shake until chilled and double-strain into a double old-fashioned glass filled with ice or over a large ice cube. Top off with ginger beer and garnish with the lime wedge and blackberries.

SUMMER QUARTET

The Summer Quartet made its debut on the menu at Momofuku Ssäm Bar and Momofuku Ko under the category listed as Quartet. Momofuku bar director John deBary says, "I'm really drawn to four-ingredient, equal-part drinks like the Last Word, Naked and Famous, and Corpse Reviver No. 2, so at Momofuku we've created a category to feature these."

Sotol is an herbaceous, rustic spirit produced in Chihuahua, Mexico, distilled from the sotol plant, with notes of citrus and smoke. "One hallmark of these drinks is that they take intensely flavored ingredients and manage to balance each other out," says deBary.

MAKES 1 DRINK

¾ ounce Ocho Cientos Blanco sotol

¾ ounce Amaro Montenegro

¾ ounce St. George raspberry liqueur

¾ ounce freshly squeezed lime juice

Pinch of kosher salt

Combine all the ingredients in a cocktail shaker filled with a large ice cube. Shake until chilled and strain into a chilled double old-fashioned glass.

"I find that amaro is one of the most food-friendly things to drink, whether it is in a cocktail or on its own. Salt, found in food or mixed into a cocktail, transforms the bitterness into a beguiling sweetness that really adds to the gustatory experience. Also, bitterness stimulates digestion, so what more can you ask for in a beverage?"

—JOHN DEBARY
Momofuku, New York, New York

AMARO EX MACHINA

When I first heard about something called an amaro machine, I pictured a steampunk-like serving device or a Rube Goldberg contraption with many moving parts. The amaro machine is a featured attraction at the Sportsman's Club, a neighborhood bar in Chicago's Ukrainian Village, which opened in December 2013 at the same address of a bar of the same name that was a favorite gathering place for Polish immigrants. The machine itself looks like the kind used to serve chilled shots of Jägermeister, but the one at Sportsman's began life as an Averna machine. Two bottles of booze are inverted into slots at the top of the device and a stirring mechanism keeps the solution in constant motion over a cold plate until a shot pours out from a tap in the front.

Wade McElroy, the managing partner and beverage director of Sportsman's Club, says that the original house blend that christened the amaro machine was a mix of Averna, Cynar, Zucca, and Cocchi Americano Rosa. Each day, the bartender on duty uses a Solera method to replenish the brew, adding new amaro, sherry, fortified wine, or even cold-brew coffee, never letting it run out. McElroy notes, "Over the past couple of years the blend has gained complexity each and every day with the addition of new ingredients compounding with all the previous brands." Sherry is a particular favorite with the staff. "It complements the amaro in such an awesome way, adding a rich sweetness that fills out the bitter amaro blends," McElroy says. You can take your amaro as a shot, served neat, on the rocks, or topped with soda. McElroy likes it on the rocks with a swath of orange peel, and the amaro machine has been an essential part of the bar's five-dollar Low Life promotion: a Miller High Life served with a shot of whiskey or amaro.

THISTLE AND WEEDS

The lighter, wine-based Cardamaro plays nicely as an aperitif. The 100-year-old Bosca family recipe infuses the wine with cardoon and Roman thistle, among other botanicals, and it is then aged in new oak barrels, resulting in a softer, sherry-like amaro. The Amara Amaro d'Arancia Rossa, made with blood oranges from Sicily, is on the sweeter side of the bittersweet spectrum and brings a pop of citrus-forward brightness to the drink.

....

Combine the Cardamaro, Amara, and bitters in a mixing glass filled with ice. Stir until chilled and strain into a highball glass filled with ice. Top off with Prosecco and garnish with the orange zest.

MAKES 1 DRINK

1 ounce Cardamaro Vino Amaro

½ ounce Amara Amaro d'Arancia Rossa

2 dashes grapefruit bitters

Prosecco or sparkling wine

Garnish: orange zest

THE VELVET DITCH

Jayce McConnell is now the head bartender at Edmund's Oast in Charleston, South Carolina, but when I first met him he was behind the stick at his first bartending job at John Currence's Snackbar in Oxford, Mississippi. "It was a great first experience—wonderful customers, passionate coworkers, and a welcoming small town vibe. Oxford is a great place to live, but it's an easy place to get comfortably stuck for a while, which is why the locals have given it the nickname the Velvet Ditch."

It's fitting, then, that his homage to his Oxford days has a "wonderful, velvety mouthfeel" thanks to the mix of citrus and confectioners' sugar that settles on top of the drink, adding body. The resulting frothy head on the drink becomes a landing pad for delicate garnishes, like the freshly grated cinnamon that closes out the drink with a warm burst of aromatics.

....

Combine all the ingredients except the garnish in a cocktail shaker filled with ice. Shake until chilled and double-strain into a chilled coupe or cocktail glass. McConnell advises to start pouring low and close to the glass, then carefully raise your shaker and strainer at least a foot over the glass to help created a nice layer of foam on the surface of the cocktail. Garnish with freshly grated cinnamon.

MAKES 1 DRINK

1½ ounces Damoiseau VSOP rhum agricole

¾ ounce Cynar

½ ounce Amaro Montenegro

1 tablespoon confectioners' sugar

2 lemon wedges

5 dashes grapefruit bitters

Garnish: freshly grated cinnamon

THE VICTORIAN

MAKES I DRINK

2 ounces Damrak gin

½ ounce Tempus Fugit Spirits Fernet del Frate Angelico

½ ounce Varnelli Amaro Dell'Erborista

¼ ounce Sirop de Capillaire (recipe follows)

2 or 3 dashes wormwood bitters (see Note)

Garnish: lemon zest

This bold and bitter creation comes from Alex Bachman, a partner and bartender at Chicago's Billy Sunday, home to one of the greatest selections of rare and vintage amari in America. The Victorian is a tribute to "the wonderful Vicki Wadick," a regular at a southern Sonoma County, California, bar where Bachman worked around 2011. "She used to carry around a laminated piece of paper with names of amaro on it to check off as she tasted through them. Naturally we became fast friends."

Combine all the ingredients except the garnish in a mixing glass filled with ice. Stir until chilled and strain into a chilled coupe or cocktail glass. Garnish with the lemon zest.

NOTE Cocktail Kingdom and Dillon's both make a commercial wormwood bitters that you can purchase online. Or, you can make your own using Bachman's recipe: In a glass container, combine 3 cups high-proof vodka, 8 tablespoons dried wormwood, the zest of ½ lemon (cut into strips), 1 tablespoon grains of paradise, 1 tablespoon dried horehound, 1 teaspoon dried angelica root, 1 tablespoon juniper berries, and 1 cinnamon stick. Cover and allow to steep, shaking regularly, for 2 to 3 weeks. Strain through a fine-mesh sieve with wet cheesecloth and discard the solids. Then decant the liquid into bitters bottles. The bitters will last indefinitely, but are best used within a year.

SIROP DE CAPILLAIRE

MAKES APPROXIMATELY 2½ CUPS

1 cup water

2 cups granulated sugar

½ ounce gum arabic

3 tablespoons dried maidenhair fern

2 or 3 drops orange blossom water

In a medium saucepan over medium heat, bring the water, sugar, and gum arabic to a simmer, stirring the mixture occasionally to dissolve the sugar and gum arabic. At the first crack of a boil, remove from the heat.

Place the dried fern in a glass container with a lid and pour in the hot syrup to cover it. Allow to steep in the refrigerator for 24 hours.

Strain the syrup into a new glass jar with a lid and discard the solids. Stir in the orange blossom water. The syrup will keep in the refrigerator for up to a month.

THE WATERFRONT

There are three cocktails at Prime Meats that have been on the menu since day one: the Manhattan, the old-fashioned, and the Waterfront. This "pretty aggressive highball" created by Damon Boelte packs in three ounces of Fernet. "It has the most Fernet-Branca in a cocktail in the cocktail world. No one will ever be able to beat it without it just being too bitter."

The drink started off when Boelte was working at LeNell's, the now shuttered but still beloved Brooklyn liquor store. "It was a bartender's dream," remembers Boelte, telling me about LeNell's open cabinet policy to encourage staffers to taste the "rare, weird stuff from [the owner's] travels," and how David Wondrich taught him how to make a Blue Blazer in the kitchen of the store.

When he added it to the menu at Prime Meats it was meant to be an industry drink, but it caught on with customers. "It was sent back a lot. It's the only drink I made sure all the servers offered a verbal disclaimer to customers. It's every fucking bold flavor I can pour into a drink. That's really how it came about. It's a medicinal, bitter, and minty Dark and Stormy. The darkest Dark and Stormy."

MAKES 1 DRINK

2 ounces Fernet-Branca

1 ounce Branca Menta

½ ounce freshly squeezed lime juice

Ginger beer

Garnish: lime wedge and mint sprig

....

Build the Fernet-Branca, Branca Menta, and lime juice in a highball glass filled with ice. Top off with ginger beer and stir. Garnish with the lime wedge and mint sprig.

WHITE NEGRONI

MAKES I DRINK

2 ounces London dry gin

1 ounce Lillet Blanc

¾ ounce Suze

Garnish: lemon zest

When a Negroni variation doesn't use Campari and bypasses the equal parts ratio of the classic cocktail formula, can it still be called a Negroni, if not in name, then in spirit? What if it isn't even red? In the case of the White Negroni, which also travels under the title Negroni Bianco and originated in 2002 with London bartender Wayne Collins, the spirit of the drink is there—herbal, gin-forward, bittersweet—but its complexion is altered. The bitterness is brought on by Suze Saveur d'Autrefois, a French, gentian-based aperitif liqueur created in 1885 but only recently available in America. (I picked up my first bottle from a grocery store in Cognac, France, and checked it through in my suitcase.) Many bartenders have continued to put their own twists on Collins's original cover, with other new-to-the-States quinquinas and liqueurs like Salers, Bonal, or Avèze standing in for Suze, and the popular Cocchi Aperitivo Americano stepping in for the Lillet Blanc.

Combine the gin, Lillet, and Suze in a mixing glass filled with ice. Stir until chilled and strain into an old-fashioned glass filled with ice or a chilled coupe or cocktail glass. Garnish with the lemon zest.

YESTERDAY, TODAY, AND AMARO

MAKES 1 DRINK

2 ounces Wild Turkey 101 rye

½ ounce Cynar

¼ ounce Averna

¼ ounce Bénédictine

Lemon zest

One of the showcase dishes at Mike Solomonov and Steve Cook's Philadelphia restaurant Abe Fisher is a large-format, Montreal-style smoked short-rib platter. This is a dish that will have most customers pleading for a glass of amaro to help push them through to the bitter end, and beverage director Brian Kane makes sure his bar is stocked with plenty of bottles to answer that call. "The name pays homage to the history of passing down recipes for amari production from one generation to the next," says Kane. The drink is also a nod to the classic Manhattan, swapping in amaro for sweet vermouth. Kane continues, "Cynar is used for its notes of bitter orange, cocoa, and caramel, along with a bright acidity. The Averna brings cola, coffee, and vanilla, together with notes of angelica and lemon from the herbaceous Bénédictine, to create a flavor reminiscent of a complex and delicious vermouth. There are very few ingredients behind the bar that provide as much character in such small doses as amari. This drink seeks to introduce the exotic by showcasing it in a familiar setting."

Combine all the ingredients except the lemon zest in a mixing glass filled with ice. Stir until chilled and strain into a chilled coupe or cocktail glass. Express the lemon zest over the surface of the drink and discard.

ZUCCA FOR LOVE

Kavalan, the Taiwanese whisky maker that's been taking home some of the spirits world's most prestigious awards, invited a small group of American writers, including myself, to visit the distillery in Yuanshan in Yilan County. On our last night in Taipei, we were able to convince our hosts to add a visit to Ounce, the speakeasy-style bar tucked behind a nondescript door in the back of an espresso bar, to the itinerary. Exhausted from our busy schedules and still jet-lagged, most of my traveling companions went back to the hotel after one drink. But I hung back and caught up with head bartender Payman Bahmani, whom I knew from his days at PDT in New York, and bar manager Adam Robinson, an expat from Portland.

Just as I was about to call it a night, Ounce owner, Yee-Hung Soong, dropped in. Knowing my love of cats (I guess that sort of information travels with you), he took me around to several nearby bars to show off some of Taipei's finest bar cats. I was not disappointed. Bahmani and Robinson, who have both since moved on from Ounce, put together a drink to mark the occasion using one quintessentially Taiwanese ingredient, passion fruit, which, Bahmani discovered, "goes surprisingly well with amaro."

MAKES 1 DRINK

1 ounce Zucca Rabarbaro amaro

1 ounce Del Maguey Vida mezcal

½ ounce Vanilla Syrup (recipe follows)

½ ounce freshly squeezed lime juice

1 whole passion fruit (inside scooped out, including seeds) or ¾ ounce passion fruit purée

Garnish: lime wheel

Combine all the ingredients except the garnish in a cocktail shaker filled with ice. Shake until chilled and double-strain into a chilled coupe or cocktail glass. Garnish with the lime wheel.

VANILLA SYRUP

Combine all the ingredients in a medium saucepan and bring to a simmer over medium heat, stirring occasionally to dissolve the sugar. At the first crack of a boil, remove from the heat. Let cool completely, then refrigerate the syrup in a glass jar with a lid for 24 hours to allow the vanilla flavor to infuse. Strain into a glass jar or bottle with a lid and discard the solids. The syrup will keep in the refrigerator for up to a month.

MAKES APPROXIMATELY 1½ CUPS

1 cup water

1 cup sugar

3 vanilla beans, halved lengthwise and seeds scraped out (use both pod and seeds)

50/50s

When ubiquitous shots of Fernet-Branca become the norm and the bartender's "secret handshake" becomes a public high five, then it's only natural that bartenders take their shots game to the next level. The birth of most of these 50/50 spirit-amaro shots started as shift drinks from bartenders. A 50/50 can be a hail-fellow-well-met welcome to someone in the industry when they darken the door of your bar, a mid-shift pick-me-up, something shared with a regular when you present the check, or an end-of-the-night ritual.

Typically a 50/50 is just that: a composed shot of equal parts from two different bottles poured into a glass. I've had some of these shots just like that, as intended, while at bars like the NoMad my Maserati (mezcal and Ramazzotti) was first stirred over ice and then strained into a chilled glass. But would you expect anything less from such an elegant bar? A few of these shots aren't exactly equal parts, and some get a little fancy with their expressions of citrus zest. And just how much is a shot exactly? Brooklyn bartender Damon Boelte says, "I don't think a shot should be something you should choke on. Unless it's an ounce I always two-step my shots. An ounce-and-a-half shot is just about right for everyone."

CHILE-CHOKE

¾ ounce Ancho Reyes ancho chile liqueur

¾ ounce Cynar

Created at The Dawson restaurant in Chicago's West Town by Dogma Group partner Clint Rogers when he was tending bar there.

CIA

1 ounce Cynar or Cynar 70

1 ounce Laird's Bonded Apple Brandy

1 dash Angostura bitters

The CIA, from Tonia Guffey, bar manager at Brooklyn's Dram, started with Fernet. "I am a huge fan of Fernet-Branca. I have three Fernet bikes, a tattoo, and my twenty-ninth and thirtieth birthdays were even sponsored by Fernet." But looking for a change of pace, she started drinking Cynar. She missed the higher-proof kick of Fernet-Branca, so she went looking through her backbar for something to spike her Cynar. And that's when a bottle of Laird's 100-proof bonded apple brandy was put into service. "I knew I wanted overproof and I knew I wanted something pretty inexpensive that I could drink without feeling bad. And that was Laird's bonded. I added a dash of Angostura 'cause I am fancy like that, and because cinnamon and apples are a natural pairing, and it turned out to be really fucking tasty." Guffey can take the CIA to the next level with Cynar 70, the 2015 release that's double the alcohol content of the original.

FERRARI

¾ ounce Fernet-Branca

¾ ounce Campari

No one stepped up to claim ownership but rumor has it that this speedy shot hails from San Francisco, which makes sense, considering the Fernet-Branca. And like a Ferrari at a stoplight, you can't help but pause to admire it.

FULL MONTE

¾ ounce blanco tequila

¾ ounce Amaro Montenegro

1 dash Bittermens Hopped Grapefruit bitters

One of the favorite house shots served at Amor y Amargo in New York.

HEADS OR TAILS, YOU DRINK

When it comes to amaro-related collectible promotional items, the only thing that comes close to topping Underberg's leather belt with Underberg "bullets" is the Fernet-Branca challenge coin. Modeled on morale-boosting military challenge coins, these hefty, silver dollar–sized colored coins are issued every year throughout the United States. They have the Fernet-Branca logo in black, red, and gold on one side with "Year of Branca" and "Milano," and the other side of the coin features a particular city, the year, and a graphic symbolizing the featured city (an El train car for Chicago, the city skyline for New York, the Hollywood sign for Los Angeles). There are also limited-edition graphics released in honor of events like Tales of the Cocktail or a regional chapter of the United States Bartenders' Guild. These coins are handed out to bartenders or industry insiders by Fernet-Branca brand ambassadors, and as Fernet-Branca describes it, "Their lucky owners would never be parted from them." Per tradition, the coin must be carried on your person at all times. When you place his or her coin on the bar, all others in possession must also show their coins. If the challenge is met, the original person producing their coin must buy the round. If someone is unable to show a coin, then he or she buys the round of Fernet-Branca shots.

The first rule of the Fernet-Branca challenge coin club is . . . you must have a coin. I found out the hard way a few years ago when on a rainy Friday afternoon I stopped by the NoMad Bar for a drink. I was the only customer at the bar but was soon joined by my friend Rocky Yeh, who was in town from Seattle, and bartender Chris Lowder. After the first round of drinks, there was a brief pause, then Yeh slapped his challenge coin on the bar, quickly followed by Lowder echoing the motion with his own coin. They both looked at me with glee, knowing the round of Fernet shots were going to be on me. They were both shocked when I told them I didn't have a coin. Rocky, sort of embarrassed on my behalf, picked up the round and shook his head, "I can't believe Mr. Bitters doesn't have a Fernet coin." I was able to correct that mistake and now have one in my possession. So watch out, bartenders—the next round just might be on you.

HARD START

¾ ounce Fernet-Branca

¾ ounce Branca Menta

One of my all-time favorite 50/50s and one I've witnessed travel by name across New York bars is Damon Boelte's Hard Start. "Not that I like to promote drinking on the job or anything," Boelte said when remembering its origin, "but I was working brunch one day at Prime Meats with our old general manager, Bill Mann. It was kind of slow and I was probably a little hungover." Mann suggested a shot of Fernet-Branca to help bring them back to life, but as Boelte remembers, "Sometimes, early in the day, Fernet can be kind of aggressive." Taking a cue from his own cocktail, the Waterfront (page 207), he cut the shot with Branca Menta. "We take it and we're like, 'Bam! That's really good.'" Mann agreed, and upon reflection, the name of the drink and the first of many shots was born. "Bill said, 'You know when your battery is dead and you've got to roll down the hill and pop the clutch?' And I was like, 'Yeah, a hard start.' And that's the name of that drink."

One of my proudest accomplishments was introducing Fernet's Count Eduardo Branca, the sixth generation of his family to make fernet, to this Brooklyn tribute to his family's product. After giving me a personal tour around the historic Fratelli Branca Distillerie in Milan, we ended up in a room outfitted with a bar stocked with all of their products. "I'm not a bartender, but may I offer you a drink before you leave?" It was still before noon and the sunlight was spilling into the saffron-colored room, but Branca helped set the mood by turning on the neon Fernet-Branca sign that hung over the bottles behind the bar. Seeing bottles of Fernet-Branca and Branca Menta side by side meant only one thing, and I asked the count if he had ever had a Hard Start. And with that, as he poured equal parts of his family's namesake spirits into our glasses, I had inadvertently sent a bitter boomerang all the way from Carroll Gardens to Milan. He winced watching me shoot it back. "You Americans love your shots. In Italy we still sip fernet."

JÄLORT

¾ ounce
Jägermeister

¾ ounce Bäska
Snaps med Malört

Austin bartender Dennis Gobis was doing inventory with the varsity team at the 2015 Portland Cocktail Week when they uncovered a bartender's version of the Ark of the Covenant: a cache of eighteen bottles of Jeppson's Malört and eighteen bottles of Jägermeister. Back home, he's making them with Bäska Snaps. "They share some botanicals, yet the citrus in Bäska Snaps complements the heavier botanicals in Jägermeister."

THE JIMBO

¾ ounce Old
Overholt rye
whiskey

¾ ounce Amaro
Meletti

"The Jimbo is one of my favorite examples of the double helix that is bar life and bar lore," says Jimmy Palumbo, recalling the early days of his namesake amaro shot. Palumbo is now working at New York's Up and Up, but at the time of the Jimbo's creation he was behind the stick at Extra Fancy. He lived across the street from the bar and would often end up spending late nights developing the drink menu after they closed. After these late-night rounds of R&D, he'd retire to his rooftop across the street and enjoy one last drink as he watched the sun rise ("a nightcap, minus the night").

On one of these occasions, home-bar pickings were slim. "We had basically drunk everything but a bottle of Rittenhouse rye and a bottle of Meletti Amaro." That combination came back to him a few days later at Extra Fancy, when a pack of twentysomething women spilled into the bar seeking "a round of shots, whiskey shots, but not sweet, and not, like, sour, but strong, but not too strong." Seeking to quickly please them and send them on their way, he reached for the Rittenhouse and Meletti. After knocking them back, he was greeted with: "That. Was. Fucking. Amazing. What do you call that?" On cue, Palumbo's colleague leaned in and put his arms around his shoulders. "It's called the Jimbo. And ladies, this is Jimbo."

"And there it happened. A few days later we poured shots for some close industry friends. They loved it, and from that point on it became the house industry shot. We eventually changed to Overholt because the Rittenhouse was getting people a bit too tipsy at the rate we poured them out." While the drink is typically just poured into a glass, Palumbo has a specific technique. "The Meletti has to be poured first and then you float the rye on top. Now, is that to say that I always make sure to float the rye? Not even close." Looking back, he admits, "It's just been a fun little thing watching this grow from a serendipitous accident on my rooftop into something that people are calling for in other cities."

MAGARI

On the menu at Barnacle in Seattle, David Little describes the Magari ("I wish" in Italian) as tasting like a "fancy Girl Scout cookie."

¾ ounce Branca Menta

¾ ounce Meletti Cioccolato liqueur

MALORI

The house shot at Slippery Slope in Chicago's Logan Square features the Windy City's infamous bitter liqueur.

¾ ounce Jeppson's Malört

¾ ounce Campari

MASERATI

Mother of Pearl's Jane Danger is the mother of this invention, which she batches at her bar and pours by the glass.

1 ounce Amaro Ramazzotti

½ ounce mezcal

NAR NAR

A favorite of Wade McElroy at the Sportsman's Club in Chicago's Ukranian Village.

¾ ounce Amaro Nardini

¾ ounce Cynar

NEWPORT

When you want that menthol-smooth sensation of a Newport cigarette in your shot glass, Amor y Amargo's Sother Teague has you covered.

¾ ounce mezcal

¾ ounce Branca Menta

SCHATZ, BRO

1 ounce Pierre
Ferrand 1840
Cognac

½ ounce
Amaro Nonino
Quintessentia

Orange zest,
expressed and
discarded

When Chris Lowder was behind the bar at Amor y Amargo, he might've welcomed you with a big bitter squeeze in the form of his favorite house shot, Shatz, Bro!

SPAGHETTI

¾ ounce Strega

¾ ounce
Cappelletti
Vino Aperitivo
Americano Rosso

My own contribution that, until now, has only been known within the confines of my apartment. Sounds weird, but I promise it tastes like a watermelon Jolly Rancher.

ZUCCA JOE

¾ ounce Zucca
Rabarbaro amaro

¾ ounce coffee
liqueur, preferably
New Deal

One of my favorite names of the bunch, from David Little at Barnacle in Seattle.

CHAPTER 6

MAKING YOUR OWN

AMARO

GIVE DIY A TRY

The goal of making your own amaro at home doesn't have to be an attempt to make a clone of Fernet-Branca or Averna. Instead, it presents the opportunity to explore the tradition of amaro by putting your own personal spin on a DIY blend. Many amaro producers have more than one hundred years of experience making herbal liqueurs, so it's unlikely your home brew is going to knock those historic bottles off the top shelf of your home bar. That being said, making your own postprandial elixirs is a great opportunity to dive a little deeper into the subject while making the most of the seasonal, regional ingredients around you. I encourage you to treat the recipes for these four seasonally inspired amari as templates, a launching pad for you to adjust, tweak, and ultimately make your own. I recommend serving these homemade amari neat in a chilled glass or with a couple of ice cubes.

These recipes are presented for your own enjoyment, or to share with like-minded, amaro-loving friends. When you make your own amaro, a number of factors can affect the consistency from batch to batch. Tempus Fugit Spirits' John Troia reminds us that "the variables can be dizzying when you're dealing with organic materials." It takes professionals months, and often years, of trial and error to achieve something they would even consider selling at a commercial level. But don't let that buzzkill reminder dissuade you—after all, people have been making (if not selling) their own house blends of amaro in Italy for centuries. So let's make some amaro!

BITTER BASICS

While they share similar production methods, the distinction between aromatic bitters like Angostura and Peychaud's and amari is that the former are classified as nonpotable while the latter are potable. Nonpotable bitters are not meant to be consumed on their own, but instead used as a flavoring agent, dispatched in dashes and drops. These are aromatic, high-proof solutions (around 45 percent alcohol) and sometimes lightly sweetened. Amari fall under the category of potable bitters. They usually have lower alcohol, from 16 to 40 percent, and are intended to be consumed as an alcoholic beverage.

PRODUCTION METHODS

The general formula for making amaro starts when herbs and botanicals, typically dried, are selected for the blend and crushed to help release their intrinsic properties. These crushed herbs, spices, roots, barks, and botanicals are then steeped for a desired period of time in a water or alcohol solution. After they're filtered, water and sugar are added to the final infusion.

The easiest way to get started, and the method used in the recipes that follow, is to combine all of the ingredients in one vessel in a high-proof or overproof neutral alcohol and allow to steep for a period of time. This solution is filtered and then sugar and water are added and the solution rests for a continued period of time until it is ready to drink. With these recipes, you'll be ready to try your homemade amaro after five weeks of patiently waiting, but you could also tuck your bottles away for additional weeks or months for extra bottle aging. You could even use a small barrel procured online or from a friendly nearby distillery to barrel-age your amaro for even more depth of flavor (and darker color).

A more advanced method of making your own amaro is to create individual tinctures of each ingredient and then blend them together to your liking. To make a tincture, fill a glass jar a quarter of the way with your desired ingredient, then add a high-proof or overproof vodka to cover the solids. Depending on the ingredient, the tincture can take hours, days, or up to a week or more to reach peak flavor. Monitor the progress by observing the color changes in the solution. This is then strained and what remains is an undiluted and unsweetened high-proof solution of a single flavor.

HERBS, SPICES, AND BOTANICALS

It's true, you're not going to find cinchona bark next to the jar of McCormick's ground cinnamon at your neighborhood grocery store, but don't let that scare you away. Sourcing most of these exotic roots, barks, and botanicals can seem like the most daunting part of operation Make Your Own Amaro, but everything can easily be procured online. If you live in a bigger city or college town, you can scan the shelves at a natural health store to secure some of these ingredients, but my go-to outlet remains Dandelion Botanical Company in Seattle. Whether you stop by in person, call them on the phone, or order online, the knowledgeable owners, Mary Cassinelli and Brian Kern, are friendly and patient and will help you gather everything you need to get started.

Look for roots and barks that are cut and sifted, and avoid using them in powdered form. And unless noted, most herbs and spices you'll be using will be dried. You'll just need a small amount of each one to get started, so they're pretty affordable, even factoring in shipping costs.

You can't have amaro without bringing on the bitter, and the following roots and barks make up the agents that will amp up the bitterness level as well as the toniclike properties behind amaro's reputation as an end-of-meal lifesaver.

BITTERING AGENTS

Angelica root (*Angelica archangelica*)

Burdock root (*Arctium lappa*)

Cherry tree bark (*Prunus serotina*)

Cinchona bark (*Cinchona succirubra, Cinchona calisaya*)

Fringe tree bark (*Chinonanthus virginica*)

Galangal root (*Alpinia galangal*)

Gentian root (*Gentiana lutea*)

Licorice root (*Glycyrrhiza uralensis*)

Quassia bark (*Quassia amara*)

Wormwood (*Artemisia absinthium*)

BASE SPIRIT

You will need a high-proof or overproof neutral spirit to get the most from your botanicals over a set period of time before they lose their effectiveness. Everclear comes in two versions—151 proof (75.5 percent alcohol) and 190 proof (95 percent alcohol)—but its sale is prohibited in many states. Boyd and Blair potato vodka out of Pennsylvania is a "professional proof" expression at 151 proof (75.5 percent alcohol) but has limited availability. I've had the best luck sourcing Devil's Springs 151-proof (75.5 percent alcohol) vodka from the great state of New Jersey. If you have difficulties sourcing 151-proof vodka, Absolut, Smirnoff, and Stolichnaya all have 100-proof vodkas in their portfolios—just don't use anything that's less than 100 proof.

GEAR

You'll need to have a mortar and pestle (or make due with a rolling pin), a cutting board, a chef's knife and a paring knife, and a vegetable peeler to prepare the fruit, herbs, barks, spices, and botanicals.

For the glass jars to hold your amaro during the maceration process, I recommend using 32-ounce or 64-ounce Mason jars with lids. Be sure to wash with hot water before using them.

To strain your amaro solution, you'll need a large fine-mesh strainer and a lot of cheesecloth. A large funnel is helpful for transferring from jar to jar; use a small funnel for decanting into bottles.

BOTTLES

You can find a wide assortment of handsome bottles to hold your finished amaro at any number of home-goods stores, craft stores, or online. If you're ordering in bulk, I recommend Specialty Bottle in Seattle for selection and price. You can decant your amaro into one big bottle or break it up into two or three smaller jars. I'm a fan of the flask-style glass bottles with the swing-top clamp lid that come in both 8½- and 17-ounce sizes. The same swing-top clamp lid model comes in a standard shape in sizes ranging from 8½ to 34 ounces.

AUTUMNAL AMARO

MAKES 28 OUNCES

½ cup pecans

½ cup walnuts

1 tablespoon chopped dried orange peel

1 tablespoon gentian root

1 teaspoon devil's club root

1 tablespoon cinchona bark

1 tablespoon birch bark

1 teaspoon wild cherry bark

½ teaspoon schizandra berries

Zest of 1 orange, cut into strips with a paring knife

½ cup chopped dried apple

1 cinnamon stick

3 cups high-proof or overproof vodka, or more as needed

½ cup Demerara syrup (see page 118)

Preheat the oven to 350°F. Spread out the pecans and walnuts on a baking sheet and toast in the oven for about 10 minutes, until fragrant, being careful not to let them burn. Allow to cool.

Using a large mortar and pestle, lightly break up the dried orange peel, gentian root, devil's club root, cinchona bark, birch bark, wild cherry bark, and chizandra berries.

Place all the ingredients except the vodka and Demerara syrup in a quart-sized Mason jar or other large glass container with a lid. Pour in the vodka, adding more if necessary so that all the ingredients are covered. Seal the jar and shake it. Store at room temperature out of direct sunlight for 3 weeks, shaking the jar on occasion.

After 3 weeks, strain the maceration solution through a fine-mesh strainer into a clean bowl or quart-sized jar to remove the solids, then strain the liquid through a damp cheesecloth–lined funnel into a new clean glass jar. Repeat until all the sediment has been filtered out. Squeeze the cheesecloth over the jar to release any excess liquid.

Add the Demerara syrup to the jar and stir to incorporate, then cover and shake to fully dissolve the syrup. Store at room temperature out of direct sunlight for 2 more weeks, shaking the jar on occasion.

Taste to see if the amaro is to your liking. If it's too strong, you can add more syrup or filtered water.

Using a damp cheesecloth–lined funnel, decant the mixture into one large bottle or several smaller bottles and label. Shake the bottles before using. The amaro will last indefinitely, but for optimum flavor use within a year. It's best served neat in a chilled glass or with a couple of ice cubes.

WINTER SPICE AMARO

Using a mortar and pestle, lightly break up the dried orange peel, star anise pod, anise seeds, cardamom pods, juniper berries, cloves, gentian root, pine bark, pine needles, wintergreen, and mint.

Place all the ingredients except the vodka and Demerara syrup in a quart-sized Mason jar or other large glass container with a lid. Pour in the vodka, adding more if necessary so that all the ingredients are covered. Seal the jar and shake it. Store at room temperature out of direct sunlight for 3 weeks, shaking the jar on occasion.

After 3 weeks, strain the maceration solution through a fine-mesh strainer into a clean bowl or quart-sized jar to remove the solids, then strain the liquid through a damp cheesecloth–lined funnel into a new clean glass jar. Repeat until all the sediment has been filtered out. Squeeze the cheesecloth over the jar to release any excess liquid.

Add the Demerara syrup to the jar and stir to incorporate, then cover and shake to fully dissolve the syrup. Store at room temperature out of direct sunlight for 2 more weeks, shaking the jar on occasion.

Taste to see if the amaro is to your liking. If it's too strong, you can add more syrup or filtered water.

Using a damp cheesecloth–lined funnel, decant the mixture into one large bottle or several smaller bottles and label. Shake the bottles before using. The amaro will last indefinitely, but for optimum flavor use within a year. It's best served neat in a chilled glass or with a couple of ice cubes.

MAKES 28 OUNCES

1 tablespoon chopped dried orange peel

1 star anise pod

1 teaspoon anise seeds

6 green cardamom pods

6 juniper berries

4 cloves

2 tablespoons gentian root

1 tablespoon white pine bark

1 tablespoon pine needles

1 teaspoon dried wintergreen

1 teaspoon dried mint leaves

½ cup dried cranberries

½ cup chopped dried figs

Zest of 1 grapefruit, cut into strips

Zest of 1 tangerine, cut into strips

Zest of 1 lemon, cut into strips

1 (1-inch) piece peeled fresh ginger, cut into ¼-inch slices

1 cinnamon stick

3 cups high-proof or overproof vodka, or more as needed

½ cup Demerara syrup (see page 118)

RITE OF SPRING AMARO

MAKES 28 OUNCES

1 tablespoon
chopped dried
orange peel

1 teaspoon anise
seeds

6 green cardamom
pods

1 tablespoon
wormwood

1 tablespoon
angelica root

1 teaspoon licorice
root

1 teaspoon dried
hyssop

1 tablespoon dried
hops

1 teaspoon dried
artichoke leaf

1 teaspoon dried
lemongrass

Zest of 1 orange,
cut into strips with
a paring knife

Zest of 1 lemon,
cut into strips with
a paring knife

Zest of 1
grapefruit, cut into
strips with a paring
knife

6 mint sprigs

6 fresh sage leaves

3 cups high-proof
or overproof vodka,
or more as needed

½ cup simple syrup
(page 118)

Using a mortar and pestle, lightly break up the dried orange peel, anise seeds, cardamom pods, wormwood, angelica root, licorice root, hyssop, hops, artichoke leaf, and lemongrass.

Place all the ingredients except the vodka and simple syrup in a quart-sized Mason jar or other large glass container with a lid. Pour in the vodka, adding more if necessary so that all the ingredients are covered. Seal the jar and shake it. Store at room temperature out of direct sunlight for 3 weeks, shaking the jar on occasion.

After 3 weeks, strain the maceration solution through a fine-mesh strainer into a clean bowl or quart-sized jar to remove the solids, then strain the liquid through a damp cheesecloth–lined funnel into a new clean glass jar. Repeat until all the sediment has been filtered out. Squeeze the cheesecloth over the jar to release any excess liquid.

Add the simple syrup to the jar and stir to incorporate, then cover and shake to fully dissolve the syrup. Store at room temperature out of direct sunlight for 2 more weeks, shaking the jar on occasion.

Taste to see if the amaro is to your liking. If it's too strong, you can add more syrup or filtered water.

Using a damp cheesecloth–lined funnel, decant the mixture into one large bottle or several smaller bottles and label. Shake the bottles before using. The amaro will last indefinitely, but for optimum flavor use within a year. It's best served neat in a chilled glass or with a couple of ice cubes.

SUMMER SOLSTICE AMARO

Using a mortar and pestle, lightly break up the dried orange peel, anise seeds, grains of paradise, and cinchona bark.

Place all the ingredients except the vodka and simple syrup in a quart-sized Mason jar or other large glass container with a lid. Pour in the vodka, adding more if necessary so that all the ingredients are covered. Seal the jar and shake it. Store at room temperature out of direct sunlight for 3 weeks, shaking the jar on occasion.

After 3 weeks, strain the maceration solution through a fine-mesh strainer into a clean bowl or quart-sized jar to remove the solids, then strain the liquid through a damp cheesecloth–lined funnel into a new clean glass jar. Repeat until all the sediment has been filtered out. Squeeze the cheesecloth over the jar to release any excess liquid.

Add the simple syrup to the jar and stir to incorporate, then cover and shake to fully dissolve the syrup. Store at room temperature out of direct sunlight for 2 more weeks, shaking the jar on occasion.

Taste to see if the amaro is to your liking. If it's too strong, you can add more syrup or filtered water.

Using a damp cheesecloth–lined funnel, decant the mixture into one large bottle or several smaller bottles and label. Shake the bottles before using. The amaro will last indefinitely, but for optimum flavor use within a year. It's best served neat in a chilled glass or with a couple of ice cubes.

MAKES 28 OUNCES

1 tablespoon chopped dried orange peel

1 teaspoon anise seeds

1 teaspoon grains of paradise

2 tablespoons cinchona bark

½ cup dried cherries

Zest of 2 oranges, cut into strips with a paring knife

Zest of 2 lemons, cut into strips with a paring knife

6 fresh sage leaves

6 fresh basil leaves

3 cups high-proof or overproof vodka, or more as needed

½ cup simple syrup (page 118)

CHAPTER 7

THE BITTERSWEET

KITCHEN

PUTTING THE SWEET IN BITTERSWEET

Amaro and food are intrinsically intertwined at the dining table. After the plates have been cleared and you've moved on to an espresso and are nibbling on a cookie, the bottle of amaro comes to the table. It signifies that things have come to an end, but that doesn't mean it's time to get up and leave just yet. That first sip of the herbal elixir warms you up with a bittersweet glow and soon you're not feeling as full as you did just a few minutes ago. Soon another glass is poured and the conversation continues.

On the culinary side, I wanted to take the ritual of the after-dinner amaro and combine it with the second-best part of the night: dessert. Why not combine the two and get your amaro fix in your actual dessert? Of course, that doesn't mean you can't also enjoy a tumbler of amaro with any of these bittersweet treats.

WHIPPED CREAM

MAKES APPROXIMATELY 2 CUPS

1 cup cold heavy cream

2 tablespoons confectioners' sugar

1 teaspoon amaro (optional)

It never hurts to have the ingredients for fresh whipped cream at the ready, especially when you're about to encounter a punch list of recipes for boozy and bittersweet milkshakes, ice cream sodas, affogatos, and hot chocolate. To spike your topping, just add 1 teaspoon of your favorite amaro during the mixing process.

Place the bowl and whisk from your stand mixer (or a large bowl and a whisk) in the freezer to chill for at least 15 minutes. Remove the chilled equipment from the freezer, add the heavy cream to the bowl, and whisk until the cream thickens slightly. Then add the confectioners' sugar and amaro and whisk until the cream forms stiff peaks.

CAFFÈ CORRETTO

An espresso is always a civilized way to end a meal, but the Italians have made that simple pleasure even more refined with the *caffè corretto*. Simply put, it's a "corrected coffee," improved with the addition of a splash of grappa, brandy, Sambuca, or anisette. But that other end-of-meal digestif, amaro, is the perfect partner to complement the bitter espresso. Leave the bottle right on the table so you and your guests can add a splash of amaro to your liking, but equal parts espresso and amaro works best.

MAKES 1 DRINK

1 hot espresso

1 shot amaro

Sugar (optional)

....

Spike your espresso with a shot of amaro. Add sugar to your liking, if desired.

DRUNKEN AFFOGATO

SERVES I

*1 large scoop gelato
or ice cream*

*1 shot hot espresso
(approximately
1 to 1½ ounces)*

*1 shot amaro
(approximately
1 to 1½ ounces)*

Italian for "drowned," an affogato is the simple but brilliant combination of gelato or ice cream doused in a shot of espresso. The play of hot and cold and bitter and sweet results in a simple yet delicious closer.

You can swap in a shot of amaro for the espresso for an intriguing finish that allows you to mix and match combinations like the Alpine-inspired Amaro Bràulio with a sour raspberry sorbetto or rich, chocolate gelato covered with minty Branca Menta. You can also double down and pour both a shot of amaro and a shot of espresso over your gelato or ice cream (sorbetto works best as an amaro-only affair as the espresso can clash with fruit-forward flavors).

Serve the gelato or ice cream in a chilled bowl or mug and cover with a shot of hot espresso and complementary amaro.

SPIRITED GELATO/SORBETTO AND AMARI PAIRINGS

GELATO

Caramel | Averna, Amaro Lucano, Amaro Meletti

Coffee | Averna, Amaro Lucano, Amaro Meletti

Chocolate | Fernet-Branca, Branca Menta, Amaro Lucano, Amaro Nardini, Amaro Nonino Quintessentia

Fior di latte | Averna, Amaro Nardini, Amaro Nonino Quintessentia

Hazelnut | Averna, Amaro Meletti

Mint | Branca Menta, Foro Amaro Speciale

Vanilla | Averna, Amaro Nonino Quintessentia, Branca Menta, Cardamaro Vino Amaro, Amaro Ramazzotti

SORBETTO

Blood orange | Amaro CioCiaro, Campari, Cappelletti Vino Aperitivo Americano Rosso

Cherry | Amaro CioCiaro, Amaro Bràulio, Amaro Ramazzotti

Lemon | Campari, Cappelletti Vino Aperitivo Americano Rosso, Contratto Aperitif

Raspberry | Amaro Bràulio, Amaro Ramazzotti

Strawberry | Foro Amaro Speciale

AMARO-SPIKED MILKSHAKES

You know how you sometimes think the only way you'd ever relive high school is with all of the experience and knowledge you possess as an adult? Spiked milkshakes are a somewhat (OK, very) indulgent way to indulge the sweet tooth of your youth *and* your more refined, adult palate. And adults are allowed to spike their milkshakes with booze, making these decidedly over-twenty-one affairs. This makes a decadent milkshake for one, or you can pour these into two smaller glasses if you're in the mood to share.

BRANCA MENTA COOLER

MAKES I DRINK

3 large scoops mint chocolate chip ice cream

2 ounces Branca Menta

Whipped cream (page 236)

Garnish: chocolate shavings and mint sprig

Combine the ice cream and Branca Menta in a blender and blend until smooth and creamy. Pour into a chilled glass. Top with the whipped cream and garnish with the chocolate shavings and fresh mint.

MIDNIGHT IN MILANO

MAKES I DRINK

3 large scoops chocolate ice cream

2 tablespoons malted milk powder

2 ounces Fernet-Branca

Whipped cream (page 236)

Garnish: chocolate shavings and a cocktail cherry

Combine the ice cream, malted milk powder, and Fernet-Branca in a blender and blend until smooth and creamy. Pour into a chilled glass. Top with the whipped cream and garnish with the chocolate shavings and cocktail cherry.

BRANCA MENTA COOLER

DIRTY BOULEVARDIER

BITTERSWEET SICILIAN

Combine all the ingredients except the whipped cream and garnish in a blender and blend until smooth and creamy. Pour into a chilled glass. Top with the whipped cream and garnish with the caramel drizzle and cocktail cherry.

MAKES 1 DRINK

2 large scoops coffee ice cream

1 large scoop caramel ice cream

1 tablespoon malted milk powder

Pinch of salt

2 ounces Averna

Whipped cream (page 236)

Garnish: caramel drizzle and cocktail cherry

DIRTY BOULEVARDIER

Combine all the ingredients except the whipped cream and garnish in a blender and blend until smooth and creamy. Pour into a chilled glass. Top with whipped cream and garnish with the shaved orange zest and cocktail cherry.

MAKES 1 DRINK

2 large scoops vanilla ice cream

1 large scoop blood orange gelato or sorbetto

1 ounce bourbon

1 ounce Campari

Whipped cream (page 236)

Garnish: shaved orange zest and a cocktail cherry

BITTERSWEET ICE CREAM SODAS

The American soda fountain gets an Italian makeover with these refreshing, and certainly boozy, blends of ice cream, soda, and amaro. Credit for the Campari float goes to Pam Wiznitzer of the Seamstress in New York.

CAMPARI FLOAT

MAKES 1 DRINK

1½ ounces Campari

3 ounces orange soda

1 large scoop vanilla ice cream

Build the Campari, orange soda, and ice cream in a chilled glass. Stir and serve with a straw and spoon.

AMARO ROOT BEER FLOAT

MAKES 1 DRINK

1½ ounces Amaro Ramazzotti

3 ounces root beer

1 large scoop vanilla ice cream

Build the Amaro Ramazzotti, root beer, and ice cream in a chilled glass. Stir and serve with a straw and spoon.

FERNET AND COKE FLOAT

MAKES 1 DRINK

1½ ounces Fernet-Branca

3 ounces Mexican Coke

1 large scoop vanilla or chocolate ice cream

Build the Fernet-Branca, Mexican Coke, and ice cream in a chilled glass. Stir and serve with a straw and spoon.

CAMPARI FLOAT

FERNET AND COKE FLOAT,
PAGE 246

APERITIVO ICE POPS

The next best thing to having a Campari and soda on a hot summer day. You can also try it with Aperol or Cappelletti Vino Aperitivo Americano Rosso in place of the Campari.

....

In a medium saucepan over medium heat, bring the sugar and water to a simmer, stirring the mixture occasionally to dissolve the sugar. At the first crack of a boil, remove from the heat. Stir in the orange juice, grapefruit juice, Campari, and salt. Let cool to room temperature, then pour into ice-pop molds (makes enough for ten 3-ounce molds or eight 4-ounce molds). Freeze for at least 12 hours or follow the pop mold manufacturer's instructions.

MAKES 8 TO 10 ICE POPS

½ cup sugar

½ cup water

1½ cups freshly squeezed orange juice

1 cup freshly squeezed grapefruit juice

⅓ cup Campari

Pinch of kosher salt

FERNET AND COKE ICE POPS

Sometimes it's okay to be bitter. Especially when you're enjoying the national drink of Argentina on a stick.

....

In a medium saucepan over medium heat, bring the sugar and water to a simmer, stirring the mixture occasionally to dissolve the sugar. At the first crack of a boil, remove from the heat. Stir in the Mexican Coke and Fernet-Branca. Let cool to room temperature, then pour into ice-pop molds (makes enough for ten 3-ounce molds or eight 4-ounce molds). Freeze for at least 12 hours or follow the pop mold manufacturer's instructions.

MAKES 8 TO 10 ICE POPS

½ cup Demerara sugar

½ cup water

2½ cups Mexican Coke

⅓ cup Fernet-Branca

BITTER BALLS

Rum balls have always been a little too boozy for my taste, but mellowing out the alcohol with a lower-proof amaro brings an herbal, bittersweet depth without the sting in a rich and fudgy, truffle-like ball. You can mix and match amari here, but try starting with Amaro Meletti, Amaro Lucano, or Averna. One favorite variation is to spike the dough with Branca Menta and roll the bitter balls in unsweetened cocoa powder. This recipe is adapted from Rhonda Ruckman, executive pastry chef of Herbsaint, Cochon Butcher, Calcasieu, and Pêche in New Orleans.

....

Preheat the oven to 350°F. Spread out the pecans on a baking sheet and toast in the oven for about 10 minutes, until fragrant, being careful not to let them burn. Allow to cool.

Add the toasted pecans and crushed shortbread cookies to a food processor and pulse until combined. Transfer the cookie-pecan mixture to a large bowl.

Chop the chocolate into small pieces and place in a separate bowl. In a medium saucepan, combine the cream and corn syrup over medium heat, stirring constantly, until it comes to a boil.

Pour the hot mixture over the chopped chocolate. Let it sit for a minute, then stir together until the chocolate is completely melted. Allow to cool for a few minutes, then pour the chocolate mixture over the cookie-pecan mixture, add the amaro, then stir together. Place the bowl in the refrigerator and allow to chill for 30 minutes.

Place the Demerara sugar in a small bowl. Remove the dough from the refrigerator, and using your hands or a melon baller, form the mixture into small balls, approximately 1 inch in diameter. Dredge the balls, one a time, in the sugar, turning to coat completely. Transfer each ball to a baking sheet lined with parchment paper. Continue making balls with the remaining dough.

Store in an airtight container in the refrigerator for up to a week.

**MAKES ABOUT
30 BALLS**

1 cup pecan halves

*2 cups crushed
shortbread cookies
(12 to 14 ounces)*

*8 ounces
bittersweet
chocolate*

½ cup heavy cream

*¼ cup light corn
syrup*

⅓ cup amaro

*½ cup Demerara
sugar*

AMARO-ETTI COOKIES

**MAKES ABOUT
3 DOZEN COOKIES**

*1 (7-ounce)
package almond
paste, broken into
small chunks*

1 cup sugar

Pinch of salt

*2 tablespoons
amaro*

2 egg whites

*2 cups slivered
almonds*

My sister Victoria makes a killer Christmas cookie plate. Just after Thanksgiving, she gets to work making dozens upon dozens of cookies, which she freezes then reassembles into her magnificent holiday platters containing at least ten different varieties of cookies. Being the spoiled younger brother, I get a special plate with duplicates of my favorites among the lineup. Maybe this year I'll return the favor with a plate of these Amaro-etti cookies, a take on the classic Italian amaretti cookie. For the amaro, I recommend Averna, but feel free to swap in another to your liking. This is adapted from a recipe by Grace Parisi of *Food & Wine* magazine.

....

Preheat the oven to 350°F. Line two baking sheets with parchment paper. Using a food processor, process the almond paste, sugar, and salt until very finely chopped. Add the amaro and egg whites and continue to process until smooth. It will be a very sticky, wet dough.

Using a pastry bag fitted with a ½-inch tip, pipe small, 1-inch mounds of batter onto the prepared baking sheets, leaving about 2 inches between them. Sprinkle several slivered almonds over each mound of dough.

Bake for 9 to 10 minutes, until the cookies have risen and are lightly cracked.

Remove the cookies from the oven and let the cookies cool completely on the paper. Once cooled, carefully peel off the cookies from the parchment paper. Store the cookies in an airtight container for up to a week.

BRANCA MENTA HOT CHOCOLATE

This recipe comes from Eli Dahlin, the opening chef de cuisine at Renee Erickson's Seattle restaurant the Walrus and the Carpenter (he's now the chef at the perfectly named Seattle restaurant Damn the Weather in Pioneer Square). When he first created this, Dahlin turned to Branca Menta when he was looking for a candy cane replacement. "In general, I recommend using dark amaro with other earthy, baritone flavors and offset by brighter notes like anise, orange, or mint. Considering that approach, this recipe seems a no-brainer," says Dahlin.

....

Combine the water, sugar, vanilla, dates, and orange zest in a large saucepan over medium heat and bring to a boil. Remove from the heat, cover, and allow the ingredients to infuse for at least 30 minutes, preferably longer. Strain the liquid, discarding the solids, and bring back up to a boil.

Break the chocolate into pieces and place in a large bowl with the cocoa powder. Pour about 1 cup of the hot sugar syrup onto the chocolate. Wait 1 minute, then whisk until the chocolate is melted and the mixture is homogenous and smooth. This might require more hot liquid. Continue to whisk together the liquid and chocolate, adding the liquid in 1-cup increments until all of it is incorporated. Stir in the coffee and salt.

Carefully strain the mixture through a fine-mesh sieve into a clean saucepan and bring back up to a simmer.

When ready to serve, measure out 1½ ounces of Branca Menta into a coffee cup. Pour in ¾ cup of the hot chocolate. Top with whipped cream and garnish with orange zest.

MAKES 4 TO 6 DRINKS

5¾ cups water

¾ cup Demerara sugar

2 vanilla beans, halved lengthwise and seeds scraped out (use both pod and seeds)

6 Medjool dates, halved

Zest from 1 large orange, cut into strips with a paring knife

13 ounces high-quality bittersweet chocolate

½ cup unsweetened cocoa powder

½ cup strong brewed coffee or espresso

1 tablespoon salt, or to taste

6½ ounces Branca Menta

Whipped cream (page 236)

Garnish: freshly grated orange zest

AMARO-SPIKED MULLED HOT APPLE CIDER

MAKES 6 TO 8 DRINKS

2 quarts apple cider

¼ cup pure maple syrup

2 cinnamon sticks

2 cloves

2 allspice berries

Zest of 1 orange

Zest of 1 lemon

6 to 8 ounces of your favorite amaro

This aromatic hot apple cider might just be your best friend throughout the fall and straight through to the new year. Keep a pot simmering on the stove and the spirited autumnal aroma will lure more pop-in guests. So many different amari will work here, but you can't go wrong with Averna, Amaro Nonino Quintessentia, or Amaro Lucano.

Combine all the ingredients except the amaro in a large saucepan. Bring to a boil, then reduce the heat and simmer for 30 minutes. Pour 1 ounce of amaro into a mug and top off with the mulled cider.

BARREL-AGED FERNET MAPLE SYRUP

MAKES APPROXIMATELY 64 OUNCES

8 cups pure maple syrup

4 ounces Fernet-Branca or other fernet

Every couple of months I join my neighborhood friends Ben and Marci and Shai and Susan for a gathering of the South Brooklyn Supper Club. During the holiday season, Shai and Susan presented us with bottles of Barrel-Aged Fernet Maple Syrup. It's a funky, herbal, bittersweet syrup that serves as the ultimate condiment to have on the table over a boozy brunch, and it's a great way to have that hair of the dog that bit you and eat it too—over pancakes. This recipe requires a bit of an investment, both in time and in the cost of an oak barrel (which you can source online at sites like Amazon), but the results will be worth it.

Combine the maple syrup and Fernet-Branca in a 2-liter oak barrel. Store in a cool, dry place for 8 to 10 months.

Strain the syrup through a fine-mesh sieve lined with a damp cheesecloth into a clean glass container. Using a funnel, transfer the strained syrup into glass jars or bottles with lids and label. For best quality use within a year, though it will be long gone before then.

RESOURCES

FOR YOUR BEVERAGE AND BARWARE NEEDS

BAR KEEPER SILVERLAKE
3910 Sunset Boulevard
Los Angeles, CA 90029
(323) 669-1675
www.barkeepersilverlake.com

THE BOSTON SHAKER
69 Holland Street
Somerville, MA 02144
(617) 718-2999
www.thebostonshaker.com

BULL IN CHINA
2109 NW Irving
Portland, OR 97210
(971) 888-4085
www.bullinchinapdx.com

CASK
17 Third Street
San Francisco, CA 94103
(415) 424-4844
www.caskstore.com

CASK ON COLLEGE
3185 College Avenue
Berkeley, CA 94705
(510) 788-6228
www.caskoncollege.com

COCKTAIL KINGDOM
36 West 25th Street
5th Floor
New York, NY 10010
(212) 647-9166
www.cocktailkingdom.com

THE HOUR
1015 King Street
Alexandria, VA 22314
(703) 224-4687
www.thehourshop.com

SOLE AGENT
2536 North Kimball Avenue
Apartment 4
Chicago, IL 60647
(312) 498-7030
www.sole-agent.com

SPECIALTY BOTTLE
3434 Fourth Avenue South
Seattle, WA 98134
(206) 382-1100
www.specialtybottle.com

WHISK
231 Bedford Avenue
Brooklyn, NY 11211
(718) 218-7230
www.whisknyc.com

WHISK
933 Broadway
New York, NY 10010
(212) 477-8680
www.whisknyc.com

FOR YOUR BOTANICAL NEEDS

DANDELION BOTANICAL COMPANY
5424 Ballard Avenue NW, #103
Seattle, WA 98107
(206) 545-8892
www.dandelionbotanical.com

KALUSTYAN'S
123 Lexington Avenue
New York, NY 10016
(212) 685-3451
www.kalustyans.com

SUGAR PILL
900 East Pine Street
Seattle, WA 98122
(206) 322-7455
www.sugarpillseattle.com

TENZIG MOMO
93 Pike Street, #203
Seattle, WA 98101
(206) 623-9837
www.tenzingmomo.com

FURTHER SPIRITED READING

Arnold, Dave. *Liquid Intelligence: The Art and Science of the Perfect Cocktail*. New York: W. W. Norton & Co., 2014.

Baiocchi, Talia. *Sherry: A Modern Guide to the Wine World's Best Kept Secret, with Cocktails and Recipes*. Berkeley, CA: Ten Speed Press, 2014.

Baiocchi, Talia, and Leslie Pariseau. *Spritz: Italy's Most Iconic Aperitivo Cocktail, with Recipes*. Berkeley, CA: Ten Speed Press, 2016.

Bastianich, Joseph, and David Lynch. *Vino Italiano: The Regional Wines of Italy*. New York: Clarkson Potter, 2005.

Branca di Romanico, Niccolo. *Branca: A Spirited Italian Icon*. New York: Rizzoli, 2015.

Brown, Jared, and Anistatia Miller. *The Mixellany Guide to Vermouth and Other Aperitifs*. Jared Brown, 2011.

Clarke, Paul. *The Cocktail Chronicles: Navigating the Cocktail Renaissance with Jigger, Shaker & Glass*. Nashville: Spring House Press, 2015.

DeGroff, Dale. *The Craft of the Cocktail: Everything You Need to Know to Be a Master Bartender, with 500 Recipes*. New York: Clarkson Potter, 2002.

———. *The Essential Cocktail: The Art of Mixing Perfect Drinks*. New York: Clarkson Potter, 2008.

Dietsch, Michael. *Shrubs: An Old-Fashioned Drink for Modern Times*. Woodstock, VT: Countryman Press, 2014.

Estopinal, Kirk, and Maksym Pazuniak. *Beta Cocktails*. 2011.

Ford, Adam. *Vermouth: The Revival of the Spirit that Created America's Cocktail Culture*. Woodstock, VT: Countryman Press, 2014.

Fornatale, Peter Thomas, and Chris Wertz. *Brooklyn Spirits: Craft Distilling from the World's Hippest Borough*. New York: PowerHouse Books, 2015.

Haigh, Ted. *Vintage Spirits and Forgotten Tales: From the Alamagoozlum to the Zombie, 100 Rediscovered Recipes and the Stories Behind Them*. Beverly, MA: Quarry Books, 2009.

Heekin, Deirdre. *Libation: A Bitter Alchemy*. White River Junction, VT: Chelsea Green, 2009.

Kaplan, David, Nick Fauchald, and Alex Day. *Death & Co.: Modern Classics Cocktails, with More Than 500 Recipes*. Berkeley, CA: Ten Speed Press, 2014.

McDonnell, Duggan. *Drinking the Devil's Acre: A Love Letter from San Francisco and Her Cocktails*. San Francisco: Chronicle Books, 2015.

McLagan, Jennifer. *Bitter: A Taste of the World's Most Dangerous Flavor, with Recipes*. Berkeley, CA: Ten Speed Press, 2014.

Meehan, Jim. *The PDT Cocktail Book: The Complete Bartender's Guide from the Celebrated Speakeasy*. New York: Sterling Epicure, 2011.

Morgenthaler, Jeffrey. *The Bar Book: Elements of Cocktail Technique*. San Francisco: Chronicle Books, 2014.

Muldoon, Sean, Jack McGarry, and Ben Schaffer. *The Dead Rabbit Drinks Manual: Secret Recipes and Barroom Tales from Two Belfast Boys Who Conquered the Cocktail World.* Boston: Houghton Mifflin Harcourt, 2015.

Piccinino, Fulvio. *Futurist Mixology: Polibibite, the Autarkic Italian Answer to the Cocktails of the 1930s.* Turin, Italy: Cocchi Books, 2014.

Regan, Gary. *The Joy of Mixology: The Consummate Guide to the Bartender's Craft.* New York: Clarkson Potter, 2003.

———. *The Negroni: Drinking to La Dolce Vita.* Berkeley, CA: Ten Speed Press, 2015.

Rogers, Adam. *Proof: The Science of Booze.* Boston: Houghton Mifflin Harcourt, 2014.

Rowley, Matthew. *Lost Recipes of Prohibition: Notes from a Bootlegger's Manual.* Woodstock, VT: Countryman Press, 2015.

Sanders, Dinah. *Art of the Shim: Low-Alcohol Cocktails to Keep You Level.* Sanders & Gratz, 2013.

Simonson, Robert. *The Old-Fashioned: The Story of the World's First Classic Cocktail, with Recipes and Lore.* Berkeley, CA: Ten Speed Press, 2014.

Spivak, Mark. *Iconic Spirits: An Intoxicating History.* Guiford, CT: Lyons Press, 2012.

Stewart, Amy. *The Drunken Botanist: The Plants That Create the World's Greatest Drinks.* Chapel Hill, NC: Algonquin Books, 2013.

Vicario, Renato. *Italian Liqueurs: The History and Art of a Creation.* Sansepolcro, Italy: Aboca, 2011.

Wilson, Jason. *Boozehound: On the Trail of the Rare, the Obscure, and the Overrated in Spirits.* Berkeley, CA: Ten Speed Press, 2010.

Wondrich, David. *Imbibe! Updated and Revised Edition: From Absinthe Cocktail to Whiskey Smash, a Salute in Stories and Drinks to "Professor" Jerry Thomas, Pioneer of the American Bar.* New York: TarcherPerigee Books, 2015.

ACKNOWLEDGMENTS

I'm so very grateful that the bitter band got back together for this book in the form of my talented, too-good-for-words editor Emily Timberlake, and Ed Anderson, whose photography inspires me to try to make my words on the page as memorable as his beautiful pictures.

To my publisher, Aaron Wehner, and the amazing team at Ten Speed Press, especially Lizzie Allen, Emma Campion, Michele Crim, Ken Della Penta, Jane Tunks Demel, David Hawk, Karen Levy, Ashley Matuszak, Hannah Rahill, and Daniel Wikey.

Much love to my agent, David Black, who inspires me to be a better man—on the page, and in life.

Thank you to all of the bars, restaurants, and businesses that went out of their way to let us shoot in their establishments, and made us countless drinks:

Italy: Antica Distilleria Quaglia, Antico Caffe Greco, Bar Basso, Bar Luce, Bar Sestilli, Bistrot Della Pesa, Caffe Meletti, Camparino in Galleria, Carlo e Camilla in Segheria, Distilleria Nonino, Distillerie Fratelli Branca, Distillerie Meletti, Dry Cocktails & Pizza, Galleria Campari, Gruppo Campari, Gruppo Montenegro, Harry's Bar, Jerry Thomas Speakeasy, Luca and Andrea, Mag Café, Nottingham Forest, Orsone, Radetzky Café, Rita.

New York: Amor y Amargo, Booker and Dax, Dante, Fort Defiance, Frankies 457, Grand Army, Maialino, Momofuku Ssäm Bar, The NoMad Bar, PDT, Prime Meats.

Seattle: Barnacle, Damn the Weather, Essex, Good Bar, Herb & Bitter Public House, Palace Kitchen, Rob Roy.

Chicago: Billy Sunday, GreenRiver, Lost Lake, Milk Room, Parson's Chicken and Fish, Publican, Sportsman's Club.

A big bitter thank you to all of the spirits producers who welcomed my many queries and to those who hosted me during my travels, including Francesco Amodeo, Tremaine Atkinson, Scott Blackwell, Count Eduardo Branca, Alberto Corte, Brenton Engel, Nicholas Finger, Ben Flajnik, Avery Glasser, Janet Glasser, Dave Karraker, Chiara Latella, Ann Marshall, Fairlie McCollough, Aldo Meletti, Louisa Meletti, Matteo Meletti, Mauro Meletti, Silvio Meletti, Antonella Nonino, Benito Nonino, Cristina Nonino, Elisabetta Nonino, Giannola Nonino, Luca Palmini, Luca Pedretti, Max Rudsten, Lorenzo Tamburini, John Troia, Orietta Varnelli, Francesco Vena, Leonardo Vena, Mhairi Voelsgen, and Lance Winters.

An endless debt of gratitude to this spirited crew, who always go above and beyond with their guidance, good cheer, and counsel: Alex Bachman, Talia Baiocchi, Jeff Bell, Damon Boelte, Andrew Bohrer, David Little, Jim Meehan, Katie Parla, and Sother Teague.

To the bartenders, chefs, restaurateurs, and industry friends for their continued inspiration and generosity, and in many cases, contributions to the book: Mark Allen, Nick Anderer, Dave Arnold, Payman Bahmani, Nick Bennett, Martyn Bignell, Matt Bolus, Jamie Boudreau, Chase Bracamontes, Travis Brazil, Sue Burns, Kenaniah Bystrom, Fabio Caponi, Tad Carduci, Frank Castronovo, David Chang, Ashley Christensen, Adam Chumas, Colin Clarke, Stephen Cole, Wayne Collins, Steve Cook, Eli Dahlin, Jane Danger, Natasha David, Kyle Davidson, John deBary, Nick Detrich, Tom Douglas, Billy Durney, Maggie Early, Anu Elford, Chris Elford, Justin Elliott, Renee Erickson, Frank Falcinelli, Seth Freidus, St. John Frizell, Jeff Galli, Dennis Gobis, Rebekah Graham, Tonia Guffey, Marco Haines, Chris Harkness, Graham Heubach, Bobby Heugel, Brice Hoffman, Mike Hudman, Sara Jimenez, Chris Johnson, Paul Kahan, Brian Kane, Leonardo Leuci, Sam Levy, Shawn Lickliter, Chris Lowder, Toby Maloney, Bill Mann, Jayce McConnell, Wade McElroy, Paul McGee, Matthias Merges, Guglielmo Miriello, Julia Momose, Jeffrey Morgenthaler, Jimmy Palumbo, John Parra, Taylor Parsons, Brandon Pettit, Fulvio Piccinino, Matt Poli, Marco Pompili, A.J. Rathbun, Gary Regan, Garret Richard, Adam Robinson, Leo Robitschek, Clint Rogers, Sam Ross, Matt Rudofker, Jessica Sanders, Kim Sapp, Audrey Saunders, Adam Schmidt, Charlie Schott, Jack Schramm, Joaquín Simó, Robert Simonson, Jerry Slater, Mike Solomonov, Yee-Hung Soong, Denise Spain, Amy Stewart, Maurizio Stocchetto, Jason Stratton, Joe Sundberg, Nick Talarico, Eric Tanaka, Paul Tanguay, Andy Ticer, Garrett Waddell, Anna Wallace, Levon Wallace, Molly Wizenberg, David Wondrich, Matt Woodall, Naren Young, and Evan Zimmerman.

A big Dionne Warwick-sized "That's What Friends Are For" thank you to Susan Baldaserini, Anne Bartholomew, Laurie Brown, Chris Brucia, Dave Callanan, Peter Cohen, Chris DeCrosta, Kristin Ford, Jon Foro, Jessica Gilo, Benjamin Haas, Marci DeLozier Haas, Mike Harrigan, Shai Kessler, Andrew Knowlton, Tom Nissley, Allison Renzulli, Amy Weinstein, and Crasta Yo.

Thanks to my family for their love and support: Joanne and Gary Murphy, Vicki, Bob, and Jack Adams, Gary Murphy Jr., and Ryan and Kassie Murphy. And in loving memory of my father, Herbert "Bert" Parsons, and my brother, Scott Parsons.

And Louis.

INDEX

Published in the United States by Ten Speed Press,
an imprint of the Crown Publishing Group, a division
of Penguin Random House LLC, New York.
www.crownpublishing.com
www.tenspeed.com

Ten Speed Press and the Ten Speed Press
colophon are registered trademarks of Penguin
Random House LLC.

Library of Congress Cataloging-inPublication Data
Parsons, Brad Thomas, author.
    Amaro: the spirited world of bittersweet, herbal
liqueurs with cocktails, recipes & formulas / Brad
Thomas Parsons ; photography by Ed Anderson.

First edition. | Berkeley : Ten Speed Press [2016] |
Includes bibliographical references and index.
    p. cm.
1. Cocktails. 2. Bitters. 3. Bitterness (Taste)
4. Sweetness (Taste) 5. Cookbooks. I. Title.
TX951 .P3548 2016
641.87/4—dc23
                              2016012981

Hardcover ISBN: 978-1-60774-748-2
eBook ISBN: 978-1-60774-749-9

Printed in China

Design by Ed Anderson

10 9 8 7 6 5 4 3 2 1

First Edition

"Brad Thomas Parsons's *Bitters* quickly became the definitive guide to a mysterious but essential cocktail ingredient. He's done it again with *Amaro*, a gorgeous, comprehensive, and delectable exploration of the world's bittersweet aperitifs and digestifs. Parsons's passion for the history, culture, and personalities behind these herbaceous concoctions, coupled with Ed Anderson's gorgeous photography, make *Amaro* a must-have."

—AMY STEWART, *author of* The Drunken Botanist

"I am a longtime lover of bitter Italian liqueurs. But this smart handbook has deepened my understanding of and heightened my appreciation for amaro and its kin. Read this and you will be thirsty."

—MARIO BATALI, *author of* Molto Mario

"A few things happen as you age: you start really liking yogurt, you talk about 'seeing other people,' you're willing to risk big to let out a memorable '*Bababooey!*' scream at your son's piano recital, and, fortunately, you begin to really enjoy bitters. Not only for their taste, but also because they're a panacea for the middle-aged gut. Amaro is no longer strictly a clever way to deter teenage partygoers from raiding the house bar; it's a staple ingredient, and it's about time for such a thoroughly researched and deliciously presented book on the subject. *Amaro* is complete and thirst-inducing. Two thumbs up!"

—FRÉDÉRIC MORIN *and* **DAVID MCMILLAN,**
authors of The Art of Living According to Joe Beef

"Fernet-Branca: what would we do without it? It is certainly my favorite of the amaros; some even say that it cures all known ailments and improves the humors. What a treat to read *Amaro*, a book devoted to these bittersweet aids to digestion, health, and happiness."

—FERGUS HENDERSON, *author of* The Complete Nose to Tail